Puppet Plays
for
Libraries

Puppet Plays
for
Libraries

edited by
Deanna Baran

Puppet Plays for Libraries

A Librarian's Aide Publication, October 2010

Librarian's Aide, LLC, PO Box 483, Olney, TX 76374

www.librariansaide.com

ISBN-13: 978-0-9843251-0-8

Printed in the United States of America

Contents

Editor's Note

No matter where I lived, there were puppet shows at all my favorite libraries, so when I became a librarian myself, I was pleased to discover that we were well-set in the puppet department. We had an enormous purple stage, a closet full of puppets, and a folder full of puppet plays that we performed twice a week, week after week. Once I'd been there for any length of time, however, I discovered that there were never enough puppet plays for libraries, and that the ones we did have ran the danger of overexposure by being included too frequently in the performance rotation. To help solve this, I started writing puppet plays for our library. Some were good enough for the two-year-olds to enjoy. Others were better aimed at the five-and-ups. But it was a lot of fun.

Much later, I was browsing through a small library as a patron when I saw the children's librarian give an after-school program. She sat in her chair with a storybook in one hand and homemade puppets on craft sticks in the other hand, acting out six or seven different characters and wedging the puppet-sticks in a crevice when their roles had been completed. I was impressed, and realized a library didn't need to have a large stage or a closet full of puppets in order to entertain children. Sometimes, a homemade puppet on a craft stick is all it takes. But no matter what, you can't beat a folder full of puppet plays.

Deanna Baran
December, 2009

Point of Adventure

by Daniel Munson

Tad and Cody may be any two puppets: male, female, or even animal. Rename them as needed to fit your selections and appeal to your specific audience.

Pair this puppet show with high-interest picture books about distant countries, exotic careers, famous people, or even a whimsical book about how certain items are made. As fun as stories are, this play helps remind us that the real world is a fascinating place.

Point of Adventure
by Daniel Munson

Cast:

TAD: *An energetic youth, full of imagination.*
CODY: *Another youth; Tad's friend.*

(CODY is onstage. TAD enters, his arms outstretched, moving around in circles making airplane noises.)

TAD: Zooooom! Nnnnyyyyyyyyaaaarrrrr!

CODY: Tad! What are you doing?

TAD: I'm flying. Flying to another country!

CODY: You are? When?

TAD: Right now! Look out, Cody! Here I come again! Rrrrraaaaarrrrrrrr.

CODY: Oh, you mean you're *pretending* to fly to another country.

TAD: Nope. I'm going there.

CODY: What country?

TAD: I'm going to Australia. Here I come in for a landing! Raaaaarrrrrrr! Screeeeeech!

CODY: You are too pretending!

TAD: Hey look! A kangaroo! *(TAD starts bouncing.)* Boing! Boing!

CODY: You look funny bouncing.

TAD: Boing! Boing! *(Hops around.)*

CODY: You do look kind of like a kangaroo.

TAD: I *am* a kangaroo. Kangaroos live in Australia. I know that because I've seen them there.

CODY: When did you go to Australia?

TAD: Just now.

CODY: That doesn't make any sense, Tad.

TAD: Sure it does. I read about it in a book.

CODY: A book?

TAD: Yes. Books take you places!

CODY: How can a book take you to Australia? Books don't have wings.

TAD: They don't need wings to take you places.

CODY: That sounds really strange.

TAD: When I looked at the book about Australia, and my dad read it to me, I felt just like I was there. I saw kangaroos and koala bears and all kinds of great things.

CODY: Wow.

TAD: *(Starts to rock back and forth.)* Ahoy, Matey!

CODY: What did you just say?

TAD: Rig the top sail! Hoist the anchor!

CODY: What anchor? What sail?

TAD: We're sailing on a ship across the ocean now!

CODY: We are? *(CODY starts to rock back and forth, just like TAD.)*

TAD: We're famous explorers discovering a new country.

CODY: Both of us?

TAD: Yes. Look out! Here comes a big storm.

CODY: Where?

TAD: Hold on to something so you don't get blown into the water! Whooooooooosh!

(CODY grabs TAD and they both rock back and forth as if they were on a ship.)

CODY: I don't like storms.

TAD: Whooooosh. Wheeeeewwwwwww. We're being blown back and forth. The ship is rocking!

CODY: *(Holding a hand over his mouth.)* I think I'm getting sea-sick.

TAD: Land-ho!

CODY: Just in time. Is this from another book?

TAD: Yes. I looked at a book about Christopher Columbus. He discovered America. And I felt like I was right there with him.

CODY: And we just discovered a country.

TAD: That's right. We should call it... 'Tad.'

CODY: Or 'Cody.'

TAD: Okay. We'll call this country 'Cody,' after a famous explorer.

CODY: Me? That's neat!

TAD: Now we need to protect our new country from forest fires.

CODY: Forest fires?

TAD: Did you know that sometimes they drop water on forest fires from helicopters?

CODY: Did you see them do it?

TAD: I saw lots of pictures in a book about it.

CODY: I don't think I want to get too close to a real forest fire.

TAD: Me either. That's why this was so great. It was just like being there … I watched the helicopters scoop big buckets of water from a lake, and then dump the water on a fire, but I didn't get hot. Or wet.

CODY: Can I be the helicopter pilot?

TAD: Sure! I'll scoop and drop the water. You just move a stick back and forth to fly the helicopter.

CODY: *(Makes helicopter sounds.)* Shooop shooop shooop.

TAD: To the left.

CODY: Shoop shoop shoop.

TAD: To the right!

CODY: Shoop shoop.

TAD: I've got the water!

CODY: Let's go put out the fire!

TAD: Splash!

CODY: We put out the fire! We saved our country!

TAD: Yeah! Now we can do more exploring! *(Tad 'floats' a little bit above Cody.)* Bleep bloop bleep!

CODY: What are you doing?

TAD: I'm a space explorer. Bleep bleep.

CODY: Like an astronaut?

TAD: That's right, Mission Control. I'm floating in space. Bleep. Over.

CODY: Don't tell me. You read it in a book.

TAD: It was great! From 'blast-off' to floating in space, it was…

CODY: I know… it was just like being there.

TAD: It sure was! Now I'm in a space suit and I'm floating outside the space ship. The earth looks like a blue and white ball. *(CODY starts to leave.)* Where are you going?

CODY: I'm going to the library. I want to go to new places and have adventures, too!

TAD: Wait for me. There are so many adventures in the library, I'd like to read some more!

(CODY exits. TAD moves very slowly.)

TAD: It's really hard to run in a space suit and zero gravity. Waaaaaiiiiiiit for meeeeeeee.

(TAD exits.)

Tiana Joins the Circus

by Mary Ellen Main

It's easy to get into a rut with puppet shows at the library. You may have shelves full of puppets to choose from, but it's easy to rely too heavily on just a few favorite characters. Make an effort to introduce a little bit of variety and multiculturalism into your program.

Incorporate puppets that don't look like all your other puppets. Substitute ethnic names to fit your demographic. Give everyone in your audience a puppet they can relate to—or, conversely, remind the audience that not everyone looks like they do.

Tiana Joins the Circus
by Mary Ellen Main

Cast:
BAXTER: *Quiet but friendly; skeptical of Tiana's claims.*
TIANA: *Animated.*

(BAXTER is onstage looking around for someone. TIANA enters.)

TIANA: Hi, Baxter. Sorry I'm late.

BAXTER: That's okay, Tiana. What d'ya want to do today?

TIANA: Let's go to the circus!

BAXTER: The circus? I didn't know the circus was in town.

TIANA: It is, and I'm a lion tamer. *(TIANA turns sideways and makes movements with one arm.)* Back, Simba, back!

BAXTER: But I thought you didn't like cats.

TIANA: Who, me? Tiana the Terrible?

BAXTER: Wow!

TIANA: I'm also a tightrope walker.

BAXTER: You are?

TIANA: Sure! You should see me. *(TIANA holds both arms out and walks away from BAXTER, then back again, singing a little tune.)* DA-dee-de-dee-DEE. Dee-dee-deedee-de-deedee-de-deee-dee. *(Puts arms down.)*

BAXTER: But I thought just climbing the tall slide at the park made you scared.

TIANA: *(Loudly and boldly.)* Ha ha ha! Tiana the Tightrope Walker is not afraid!

BAXTER: What happened?

TIANA: I went to the circus yesterday. *(Pauses.)* Oh, I almost forgot. I am also the ringmaster.

BAXTER: What's a ringmaster?

TIANA: Well, it's a person who tells what's going on in the circus. You know, the one who always yells, "LADIES AND GEN...TLEMEN."

BAXTER: You did that? In front of all those people?

TIANA: Of course I did. I am... TIANA THE RINGMASTER!

BAXTER: How can you be all those things, Tiana?

TIANA: It's easy! You want to be in the circus, too?

BAXTER: Me? I can't do that!

TIANA: Sure you can! I'll show you how. Come on. *(TIANA runs offstage, with BAXTER following close behind her. TIANA runs back onstage from the opposite side, with BAXTER still a few steps behind. When she returns to her original position, she stops short, and BAXTER bumps into her.)*

BAXTER: Tiana, this isn't the circus. It's the library!

TIANA: I know. Come on. It's almost time for Library Hour. Maybe we can be in the circus again today, or maybe we'll ride horses out on the ranch, or maybe we'll be bugs that crawl in the grass—

BAXTER: *(Interrupts.)* You can be all those things at the library?

TIANA: Sure you can! All you have to do is listen and pretend.

BAXTER: What are we waiting for? Let's see what we can be at the library today.
(BOTH exit.)

Curly Reads a Book

by Sarah V. Richard

Try giving your puppets a life outside of formal puppet shows. Quacky the Duck is the MC of storytime at our library. She's so popular, she gets more valentines than the librarians do.

In this play, Curly interacts with the librarian to give storytime a little more pep than merely reading a book, and you can use this as inspiration for ad-libbing your own interactions.

You can make your own Curly by jazzing up an ordinary puppet with curled-ribbon hair, or perhaps another character will emerge as your foil for (or rather, the star of) storytime. Done with enthusiasm, it will give your storytime an extra dimension of interest for both you and your audience.

11

Curly Reads a Book
by Sarah V. Richard

Cast:

LIBRARIAN: *Sitting in front of the puppet stage with a book to read.*
CURLY: *A puppet who will interact with the Librarian.*

(LIBRARIAN is sitting near the front of the stage, with a book prepared for storytime. Enter CURLY.)

LIBRARIAN: Welcome, everyone! I'm very excited to be here today.

I'm _____, and this is my friend, Curly. *(Points.)*

CURLY: *(Waves.)* Hi, everybody.

LIBRARIAN: And we just found this fabulous book here in the library. *(Holds up the book.)*

CURLY: And I had this great idea that we could read the story together! I love reading stories!

LIBRARIAN: Me too! Curly, what do you think this story is going to be about?

CURLY: Don't tell me. Don't tell me. *(Pause.)* Is the story going to be about dancing? I love dancing. *(CURLY dances.)*

LIBRARIAN: No, the story is not going to be about dancing. What else could this book be about? *(Points to picture on the book's cover.)*

CURLY: Wait, wait, don't tell me. *(Pause.)* Are we going to read about big, scary monsters? *(CURLY drops low and peers over the stage.)*

LIBRARIAN: No. Any other guesses?

CURLY: *(Scratches head.)* Hmm, how do we find out what the story is going to be about?

LIBRARIAN: Look at the pictures on the cover. Can anyone in the audience help Curly figure out what the book is about? *(Allows the audience to respond.)*

CURLY: Oh, I get it! *(Points to pictures.)* The book is about _____.

LIBRARIAN: That's right! Another way we can guess what this book is about is by reading the title.

CURLY: How can I find the title?

(LIBRARIAN points to the title and runs her finger underneath it.)

LIBRARIAN: We can find the title on the front of the book. Curly, can you read the title?

(CURLY reads the title.)

LIBRARIAN: Fantastic! Are you guys ready to read a story? *(Allows the audience to respond.)*

CURLY: Oh, I'm so excited! I love reading stories!

LIBRARIAN: All right! *(Turns the book over and opens the back page.)* Let's begin. *(Points to the last page.)* The end... *(Pause.)* Oh, dear. Something is wrong here.

CURLY: Excuse me, _____, you're reading the end of the story!

LIBRARIAN: Oh, oops! *(Holds up back of book)* This is the back of the book. I should start reading *(turns book over)* from the front of the book. Let's try it again, shall we?

CURLY: Okey dokey, smokey!

LIBRARIAN: Curly, do you mind reading the title again?

CURLY: No problem!

(CURLY repeats the title and the LIBRARIAN reads the book.)

LIBRARIAN: *(When the story is finished)* The end.

CURLY: What a great story!

LIBRARIAN: I know. Does the audience agree? *(Allows the audience to respond.)*

CURLY: I just loved the story. Do you have any more like it?

LIBRARIAN: *(Points to author's name on front of book.)* Well, the author of this book is _____. If you like this story, you might like other books he (or she) has written as well. Maybe next time we can look up the author and see if (s)he wrote any more books.

CURLY: That's a great idea. This was so much fun. I can't wait to read another story again!

LIBRARIAN: It was my pleasure.

CURLY: See you next time. 'Bye, everyone!

LIBRARIAN: Goodbye, Curly!

Goodnight, Howie

by Rachel Greene

As much as we enjoy reading to children, nothing replaces a parent taking the time to share a book with their own child. Bedtime stories aren't just a peaceful way to wind down after a stressful day, or a nice source of fond memories and bonding, or even merely a good way to encourage a child's love of reading, though they do accomplish all of those things. When parents read to children, it also helps kids develop mastery of language and encourages the development of reading comprehension as well. Use this play to remind parents to include a story in their nighttime routine, and to remind children that it's okay to use the power of imagination even when there's no one around to read the actual words.

Goodnight, Howie
by Rachel Greene

Cast:

MOM: *Strict but loving mother who is serious about bedtime.*

BRADY: *Four-year-old boy (or girl) who is brave enough to tell a story to the monster who lives under his bed.*

HOWIE: *The monster living under Brady's bed who can't sleep without a bedtime story.*

Props:

A puppet-sized book.

MOM: All right, Brady. Time for you to get under those covers and go to sleep.

BRADY: Can't we read just one story before you turn out the lights?

MOM: Not tonight.

BRADY: But you always read me a story!

MOM: It's too late. We were over at Grandma's for a long time. It is way past your bedtime.

BRADY: *(Makes begging motions.)* Please! Please! Please with a cherry on top!

MOM: *(Sternly.)* Brady.

BRADY: Oh, okay.

(BRADY lies down. Exit MOM. Make a loud "bump" sound.)

BRADY: *(Surprised.)* What was that? *(Sits up quickly and looks around. Hearing nothing, he lies back down.)*

(HOWIE, from offstage, sighs loudly two times.)

BRADY: *(Scared.)* Who's there?

(HOWIE, still invisible to the audience, starts to cry loudly.)

(BRADY sits up and looks around again.)

BRADY: *(Angrily.)* I know you're there. I can hear you crying. Come out so I can see you!

(HOWIE pops up on stage, still crying loudly.)

BRADY: *(Screams.)* Ahhh! Who are you?

HOWIE: *(Sniffling, but no longer crying.)* I'm Howie. I'm the monster that lives under your bed.

BRADY: Under my bed? Why haven't I seen you before?

HOWIE: Have you looked under your bed lately? With all of the toys and dust bunnies under there, it's a miracle I haven't gotten lost!

BRADY: *(Shamefully.)* Sorry about that. So why were you crying?

HOWIE: I can't sleep! Every night I listen to the stories your mom reads. I like to imagine I'm in the story, meeting fairies, searching for treasure, or even flying around the world. They help me fall asleep. *(Starts to cry again.)* I can't sleep without a bedtime story!

BRADY: Don't cry, Howie. I just got a really good book at the library. *(Pulls out a book.)*

HOWIE: A new library book? Oh, goody! *(Jumps up and down joyfully, then stops, suddenly serious.)* But who will read it to us?

17

BRADY: I will. I may not be able to read all the words, but I can tell what's going on in the book by looking at the pictures.

HOWIE: Okay.

BRADY: Now, you lie down and close your eyes.

(HOWIE lies down.)

BRADY: This is the story of Howie, a brave prince who got shipwrecked on a magical island. One day while he was walking through the jungle he heard a strange noise.

(HOWIE begins to snore.)

BRADY: That was fast!

(BRADY goes over to HOWIE and waves his hands in front of HOWIE's face to see if he is really asleep.)

BRADY: Howie? *(BRADY lies down with his book.)*

BRADY: Goodnight, Howie. *(BRADY starts to snore.)*

Readin' on the Range

by Nikki Loftin

Sound effects can add an extra dimension to a play. This play incorporates cowboy music to set the mood: check your CD collection to see if you have any proper hopalong cowboy music.

It also has a rattlesnake rattle. You can find real rattles for sale online, download a sound effect in MP3 format, or even try a baby's rattle. Many libraries own collections of sound effects CDs, so make use of them! Look through what you have on hand and see what other sound effects you can incorporate into storytime.

A judicious use of props will also add color to your performance. If you need a puppet-sized book, decorate a paper cover with cowboys and cacti or other Western motifs, and wrap it around a small book, such as a Beatrix Potter picture book. Props are all around you– just make sure your puppets can manipulate them!

Readin' on the Range
by Nikki Loftin

Cast:

COWPOKE: *A level-headed cowboy who loves to read.*
PARDNER: *A sillier cowboy who is afraid of snakes and does not like books.*

Props:

Four puppet-sized books.
Small tissue paper campfire.
Toy saddle.

Sound Effects:

Recordings of cowboy music (Happy Trails, Home on the Range, etc.)
Small shaker for rattlesnake.

(Play recorded cowboy music. PARDNER is on stage, resting by campfire, singing along very badly. Howl like a coyote in the distance. Drum fingers against something solid for galloping horse hoof sounds offstage.)

COWPOKE: *(Offstage.)* Whoa, Trigger!

(COWPOKE enters, carrying a stack of books)

PARDNER: Whatcha got there, Cowpoke?

COWPOKE: Oh, howdy, Pardner. I just rode in from the library with twenty head of longhorn cattle, twelve wild mustang horses, and four of the rootinest', tootinest' library books I ever laid eyes on! Just wait until you get a look-see at these here stories.

PARDNER: Never you mind giving me them books. I don't have no use for 'em. I don't like books.

COWPOKE: YOU *(gasp)* DON'T LIKE BOOKS??? That's like sayin' you don't like rodeos, or ropin' steers, or drinkin' hot chocolate around the campfire! Everybody likes books, right? *(To audience:)* Don't y'all love books?

20

PARDNER: Never did, never will. Cain't see no real use for 'em, not like my saddle, or my rope, or my spurs, or—

COWPOKE: No use for books? Whoa there, Pardner! I think you've been ridin' the range too long, and your brain's got addled. Cain't see the use for books? You joshin' me?

PARDNER: Nope.

COWPOKE: Come on, now. You really cain't think of a single reason you might want to check out a library book?

PARDNER: Well, let me see... *(Scratches head, then takes the books from COWPOKE.)* All right, all right. Okay, Cowpoke, I guess I can see a use for a few of them thar library books...

(PARDNER stacks them up and pretends to put a saddle on them.)

PARDNER: There ya go! If you stack enough of 'em up, you got a right nice place to prop up your saddle so's you can shine it— *(pretends to shine saddle and spill polish on the books; quickly wipes at the books)* —oops, I think I might have rubbed some saddle polish on a few of them thar covers—

COWPOKE: Jumpin' Jehosaphat! Pardner! What in tarnation are you doin'? You never treat a library book that way. They aren't for proppin' up your saddle, or a table, or a chair leg, or nothing. You got to take good care of library books!

COWPOKE: Now, think... cain't you come up with even one reason you might like a really good book around the campfire at night, *(dramatically)* when the coyotes are howlin', and the rattlesnakes in the brush are movin' in... *(Rattlesnake sound effect.)*

PARDNER: *(Trembling with fright.)* Coyotes? Rattlers? Quick, Cowpoke, hand me a couple of them books. Here, help me tear out some pages, so we can stoke the campfire up and scare those horrible varmints away—

COWPOKE: NO!!! You wouldn't ever burn a library book!

PARDNER: Not even to scare away a rattler?

(Rattlesnake sound effect. PARDNER jumps and screams, running over to COWPOKE.)

COWPOKE: Come on now, Pardner. Think harder.

PARDNER: Well, Cowpoke, if I can't use it to prop my saddle, and I can't throw it in the campfire… I know! Hand me a few of them thar books. *(PARDNER takes the books and constructs a small "house" with them.)* Yep… Yep. There, and there. I got it! You can make yourself a little house if you stack 'em right, and they'll keep the rain off your head. You'd need an awful lot more books if you were planning on keepin' your horse dry, though. An awful lot more. My horse, Trigger, is about this tall *(spreads hands apart to show height)*, so I figure I'll be needin' another fifty, sixty books easy.

COWPOKE: *(Exasperated.)* No, Pardner. You've got it all wrong. *(To audience:)* Does anybody know what books are good for? Anybody? *(COWPOKE allows the audience to answer.)*

PARDNER: Readin'? Oh, well, that's my problem then, I s'pose.

COWPOKE: What's your problem, Pardner?

PARDNER: Well, you see, I done spent my whole life out there on the range, ridin' fences, singin' cowboy songs, roundin' up the cattle… and I never did learn me how to read.

COWPOKE: You don't know how to read?

PARDNER: Nope, Cowpoke, I surely don't. So books aren't a bit of good to me.

COWPOKE: Now, that's where you're wrong, Pardner. You don't have to be able to read to enjoy books. Why, just look in this one...

(COWPOKE opens a book to show PARDNER.)

PARDNER: *(gasps)* Well, I'll be hogtied! There's pictures in thar! Pictures of horses, and jackrabbits, and roadrunners... and oh, my great Aunt Fannie! Look at that cowboy, sittin' on a cactus. That's hi-larious! *(Laughs, then sighs.)* I surely do wish I could read the story that goes with those pictures.

COWPOKE: Guess what, Pardner? That's what friends *(or teachers, librarians, Moms and Dads)* are for. Friends like me!

PARDNER: You?

COWPOKE: Sure! We can read this book together. You hold it and turn the pages, and I'll read the words and point 'em out to you, so you can learn 'em. *(The friends settle down by the campfire with the book, and COWPOKE begins to read.)* "Once upon a time, there were two lonely cowboys, way out on the range, with only their cattle and a couple of coyotes for company..."

(Rattlesnake sounds.)

PARDNER: *(Jumps up, sits on COWPOKE'S lap, shivering.)* Don't forget the rattlesnake, Cowpoke!

COWPOKE: "A couple of coyotes AND a rattlesnake for company..."

(Cowboy music begins, as scene ends.)

Oh, Dear. Oh, Deer!

by Cathy C. Hall

There are some very nice reindeer and Santa Claus hand puppets for sale on the internet. Housefly finger puppets are a bit more difficult to track down, but exist. But don't let the specialized cast deter you from this warm and witty play about the vagaries of language.

The illustrator has provided several models for stick puppets. Use your photocopier to increase them to a larger size and print them onto pieces of sturdy cardstock. Although you can be plain and just color them in with colored pencils or markers, consider taking a fancier route and dressing up the stick puppets with interesting buttons, bits of ribbon and trim, shiny paper, and other eyecatching scraps. Let loose your inner crafty self, take pride in your stick puppets, and no one will think them out of place.

Oh, Dear. Oh, Deer!
by Cathy C. Hall

Cast:

PRINCESS: *Just wants to bake a cake.*
DEER: *A little prone to misunderstanding.*
SANTA CLAUS: *Ready to assist.*
FLY: *Bzzzzz...*

Props:

Two-page picture book, found on p. 100.

PRINCESS: *(Onstage, upset.)* Oh, dear! I want to make a cake for the Prince's birthday, but I don't know how! Oh, dear, oh, dear, oh, dear!

DEER: *(Springs onto the stage.)* Here I am!

PRINCESS: What are you doing here?

DEER: You said, "Oh, dear." And here I am. Deer, at your service!

PRINCESS: I didn't mean that deer!

DEER: So, it's another deer you want. I'll look around... Oh, deer! Oh, de-e-e-e-r! *(DEER leaves the stage, calling for deer.)*

PRINCESS: *(Calls after DEER.)* No, no. I mean a different dear. Like "Dear Santa Claus."

SANTA: *(Arrives on stage.)* Here I am! Santa Claus, at your service!

PRINCESS: Oh, de—. Wait. I'm not going to say that again!

SANTA: Say what again?

PRINCESS: Dear.

DEER: *(Calling from below the stage.)* I'm coming, I'm coming!

PRINCESS: Oh, no! What I need is a book!

SANTA: I'll get one for you. What kind of book did you have in mind?

PRINCESS: Hmmmm. I need a book with lots of pictures.

SANTA: No problem! I'll go to the library, and I'll be back before you can say "Oh, dear!" *(Exit SANTA.)*

PRINCESS: Uh-oh!

DEER: *(Enter DEER, panting as if he's been running.)* I'm here! I'm here! *(A little annoyed.)* Deer, at your service. Again.

PRINCESS: Deer, don't go anywhere! I have a surprise for you. Now, where is Santa with that book? Santa? *(Exit PRINCESS.)*

SANTA: *(Enter, SANTA, with a picture book.)* I'm back!

DEER: Hello, Santa!

SANTA: Hello, Deer! Have you seen the Princess? She needed this book. *(SANTA sets the book on the stage, open to the two pages of pictures.)*

DEER: The Princess left to find you!

SANTA: Oh, dear! *(Exit SANTA.)*

DEER: Hello? I'm right here! *(DEER begins to mumble about people who call for a deer, then leave him all alone. Sheesh! What's a poor deer to do, etc.)*

PRINCESS: *(Enter, PRINCESS, and hears DEER mumbling.)* What did you say, Deer?

DEER: *(Exasperated.)* I'm so confused!

PRINCESS: *(Sees the book.)* Oh, my book! Now, I think we can clear this whole thing up. See, here is a deer. *(Points to picture of a deer.)*

DEER: That's me, all right! Aren't I cute?

PRINCESS: *(Looking at picture.)* Um, sure. Now, here's dear, too. *(Points to the next picture.)* See how the letter to Santa begins DEAR Santa?

DEER: Oooooooh. That dear.

PRINCESS: Exactly.

DEER: What a wonderful book!

PRINCESS: It is wonderful, isn't it, Deer? Santa found this picture wordbook at the library, so I could show you how some words sound the same but don't mean the same thing!

DEER: Hmmm. *(Thinks hard.)* Like red.

PRINCESS: Red?

DEER: Sure. Santa's hat is red. And I just read a book!

PRINCESS: That's right, Deer!

DEER: 'Bye! *(DEER begins to exit the stage.)*

PRINCESS: Wait! Where are you going, Deer?

DEER: To the library! I want to find a book about my cousin, Rudolph. *(Exits, calling from offstage.)* Poor fellow. Stuck with that red nose…

PRINCESS: *(Laughs.)* Good luck!

SANTA: *(Enter SANTA.)* Oh, I see you found the book! I hope it cleared everything up!

PRINCESS: Thanks, Santa! It was just what I needed. But I still don't know how to make the Prince's birthday cake!

SANTA: You need a book!

PRINCESS: Now, why didn't I think of that? Let's go to the library and find a "How to Make Birthday Cakes" book!

SANTA: We'll take the sled and be there in a jiffy. *(Exit SANTA and PRINCESS.)* Fly away, fly!

FLY: *(Buzzes onstage.)* Here I am! Fly, at your service! Hey! Didn't someone just call me? I know I heard someone yell, "Fly!"

What's Black and White and Red All Over?

by Deanna Baran

This was the first play I wrote for my own library. Everyone has something they love. Whether they're looking for pure entertainment or just information on an absorbing subject, your library is going to have something that's relevant to their interests. Remind them with this play that the library's not just a place full of sneezy, dusty books where you have to be quiet.

You might consider writing your own play with your specific audience in mind. How have your own young patrons discovered the library's relevancy? Or perhaps you want to place the spotlight on an underutilized part of your collection. There are countless ways to portray the library's usefulness. Libraries aren't boring places, but it's up to you to keep them from being perceived as dull.

What's Black and White and Red All Over?
by Deanna Baran

Cast:
BOY: *Wants to be a comedian when he grows up.*
GIRL: *Not very impressed with his jokes.*

BOY: Do you know what you want to be when you grow up?

GIRL: I don't know. I like animals, so I might be a vet. I like school, so I might be a teacher. Or maybe I'll become an astronaut and go to Mars. What about you?

BOY: I want to be a comedian!

GIRL: But you have to be funny to be a comedian.

BOY: I *am* funny. I've got tons of good jokes! I'd be a great comedian!

GIRL: Okay, then. Tell me a joke.

BOY: What's black and white and red all over?

GIRL: Um, I give up. What?

BOY: A newspaper! Hahahahahah! Get it? Hahahahaha!

GIRL: You're not supposed to laugh at your own jokes! You're supposed to make *me* laugh. And you didn't.

BOY: Well, hmph. It was a funny joke. I can't help it if you didn't get it.

GIRL: I got it, but I'm sure there are funnier jokes out there that you could tell.

BOY: Okay, let's try this one instead. What's black and white and red all over?

GIRL: You just did that one! It was a newspaper!

BOY: No! This is a different one. What's black and white and red all over?

GIRL: Okay, I give up. What's black and white and red all over?

BOY: A zebra with a sunburn! Hahahahahaha!

GIRL: I think that's even worse than the first one.

BOY: Awww, come on. I thought it was pretty funny.

GIRL: You're not supposed to laugh at your own jokes! You're supposed to make *me* laugh!

BOY: Well, let me try one more joke. What's black and white and red all over?

GIRL: A newspaper? A sunburned zebra?

BOY: Nope! This is a different joke. Give up?

GIRL: I give up. Tell me, what's black and white and red all over?

BOY: An embarrassed penguin! Hahahahahaha!

GIRL: Don't you know any other jokes?

BOY: Um, no.

GIRL: If you go to the library, I'm sure you could find books that are full of funny jokes and riddles. Maybe you'll have better luck being a comedian if you read some joke books.

BOY: Cool! I'll have to get some joke books the next time I go to the library. Say, do you know any riddles?

GIRL: Sure I do. What's black and white and red all over?

BOY: Hey! That's my joke! A newspaper!

GIRL: Nope.

BOY: A sunburned zebra!

GIRL: Nope.

BOY: An embarrassed penguin?

GIRL: Nope.

BOY: Then I give up. What's black and white and red all over?

GIRL: A skunk with chicken pox. Hahahahahahaha!

BOY: I think you need to come to the library with me.

An Exclusive Club

by Victoria King

Rules are no fun, but every library has them. Then again, benefits are fun, and every library has those, too. Use this play to encourage families to sign up for library cards and make use of your resources, or just make them aware of exciting upcoming events.

This play is easily modified to draw attention to a specific program, or perhaps refresh your patrons on established rules or recent changes. Perhaps your system charges for each movie checkout, or maybe you want to draw attention to an underutilized service or a brand new collection. Add a few lines, switch a few things around, *et voila!* Your audience will be informed and entertained at the same time.

An Exclusive Club
by Victoria King

Cast:
RACHEL: *Very proud of her library card.*
SAM: *Jealous of her privileges.*
LIBRARIAN: *Kind and helpful.*

Props:
A feather boa, or gaudy earrings if the puppet has ears, or some other accessory to fancy up RACHEL.

Two library cards. May be real cards from your library, or paper cut-outs, p. 104.

(*RACHEL is onstage. One library card is attached inconspicuously to her hand. SAM enters.*)

SAM: Wow! You look all dressed up! What's the occasion? Are your parents taking you to a fancy restaurant or something?

RACHEL: *(In her best high-class voice.)* Not at all, dahling.

SAM: Huh? What's wrong with your voice?

RACHEL: *(Still haughty and high-class.)* Nothing's wrong, dahling. It's just that I'm not an ordinary person anymore. I'm a member of an exclusive club.

SAM: But you're just a kid like me. Campfire Scouts isn't really what you'd call exclusive.

RACHEL: *(Still haughty.)* Silly Sam. I joined Campfire Scouts *last* year. This is different. This is special.

SAM: Oh? Then tell me about your club, Ms. Special.

RACHEL: *(Speaks normally.)* Well, they have this enormous building. It's so big, I think it has a million books in it. And I look around, show them the book I like, and they let me take it home with me. No questions asked!

SAM: Wow! They give you a book?

RACHEL: Well, they let me borrow it. I have to bring it back, in case one of the other club members wants to read it, too. But they have lots of amazing books.

SAM: So, it's a book club?

RACHEL: Well, there's more to it than that. They also have movies. Of course, they're free too, and I get to take the movies home with me, just like the books.

SAM: Free books and free movies! Wow...the only thing that's missing is free CDs!

RACHEL: Oh, yes. They have those too. And they even let me play on the computer, too. There are special computers that only club members can play on.

SAM: That sounds exciting!

RACHEL: And that's not all. During the summertime, they give us prizes for reading their books, and they even bring in special performers, like magicians and animals!

SAM: No way! Can I join?

RACHEL: I don't know. They gave me a membership card, but I don't know if they'll give one to you or not. *(Shows her library card.)* See? It even has my name on it.

SAM: Um... that's not a club membership card. That's a library card.

RACHEL: You can call it what you want to. I'm going to go home and watch one of my movies and read one of my books. And then I'll go back again tomorrow and get a different movie and a different book! See ya! *(RACHEL exits.)*

SAM: Wow... I don't have a library card. I wonder if they'll give one to me, too? *(SAM exits)*

(LIBRARIAN is onstage, making quiet working noises. SAM enters.)

SAM: Hello, ma'am! I'd like to apply for a library card! *(Worried voice.)* It's not too expensive, is it? I don't have a very big allowance. And I don't know if I'm special enough. I'm not always the best at cleaning my room, and I don't always finish my dinner, but I try hard to be good...

LIBRARIAN: Don't worry! It's very easy to get a library card.

SAM: Wow! And will I be able to borrow a book with it?

LIBRARIAN: You can borrow _____ things at one time!

SAM: Wow! _____ things! Say... so that means I can borrow movies with it, too?

LIBRARIAN: We have shelves full of movies!

SAM: Oh, how cool! And you'll let me play on the computer and check out CDs and win summer reading prizes?

LIBRARIAN: Of course! Come with me, and I'll get you a form to give to your mom or dad. If they sign it and bring it back to me, we'd be happy to give you a library card.

SAM: Thanks!

(SAM and LIBRARIAN exit.)

(RACHEL is onstage. SAM enters.)

SAM: *(With a bad British accent.)* Hello, old girl! I say, where are you off to?

RACHEL: Huh? What's wrong with your voice?

SAM: *(Still with a bad accent.)* Nothing's wrong, old girl. It's just that *I'm* not an ordinary person anymore. I'm a member of an exclusive club.

RACHEL: Oh! You got a library card, too?

SAM: *(With a bad accent.)* Right-o! *(In a normal voice.)* Want to go to the library together? There was a book I saw yesterday that I want to check out before someone else gets it!

RACHEL: You bet!

(BOTH exit.)

The Adventures of Bookman

by Mary Ellen Main

Librarians are superheroes. Who else can find "the red book about that dog" or recommend a book of scary stories that's just scary enough to be delicious, but not so scary that it gives nightmares? Library assistants and pages are superheroes, too. Who else will let you know that they just checked in a copy of that book you kept meaning to read? And any library with a children's department can think of a moment (or ten) when they wouldn't have traded their maintenance guys for a whole team of superheroes!

Libraries are places we often underappreciate (until we need to use their internet access), and the people who work in them are equally taken for granted. Remind your audience of the many ways you enrich their lives.

The Adventures of Bookman
by Mary Ellen Main

Cast:

SKIPPY: *Animated and enthusiastic.*

CARLA: *Shy but comfortable with Skippy.*

(BOTH CHARACTERS enter. SKIPPY runs ahead.)

CARLA: *(Loud whisper.)* Skippy! Skippy! What are you doing?

SKIPPY: *(Dashing back to Carla.)* I'm on the lookout for… Bookman! *(Raises one arm, looks around quickly.)*

CARLA: Who?

SKIPPY: *(Quietly.)* You know. The man who helps the librarians.

CARLA: You mean Mr. Green? He looks like my grandpa. He can't be Bookman.

SKIPPY: Watch! *(Speaks in hushed tones. Points in the distance.)* Look at what he's doing over there.

CARLA: *(Looks where Skippy is pointing.)* He's standing up and stretching.

SKIPPY: That's what he wants you to think. But look again. There he goes!

CARLA: He's taking the trash out of the trash can because it's full.

SKIPPY: Exactly! *(Speaks like a narrator.)* Mild-mannered Mr. Green sees the trash can getting full. *(More animated.)* Quickly, he stands and stretches, turning into…BOOKMAN! *(Changes voice to sound like a superhero's voice.)* "Here, *(librarian's name)*, let me get that for you."

CARLA: A superhero taking out the trash?

SKIPPY: Oh, but that's not all he does. Once I was trying to reach a book on a high shelf. *(Emphasizing words.)* I didn't even hear him walk up behind me. All of a sudden this voice said, *(changes to Bookman's voice.)* "Here, little boy. Let me help you reach that book."

CARLA: Was it Bookman?

SKIPPY: It was Bookman! *(Pauses, thinking.)* Once I saw *(librarian's name)* start to pick up a big box of books. Before I knew what had happened, Bookman had the box.

CARLA: Wow! It sounds like Bookman's a big help at the library.

SKIPPY: *(Speaks quietly and leans close to Carla.)* You wanna know a secret?

CARLA: Sure! *(Leans close to Skippy.)*

SKIPPY: Bookman doesn't work alone.

CARLA: He doesn't?

SKIPPY: No. There's a whole team of library superheroes.

CARLA: *(Very interested.)* Who are they? What do they do?

SKIPPY: That librarian *(points to one side)* puts the books in order all over the library so people can find them.

CARLA: Wow! There are superheroes everywhere at the library!

SKIPPY: There's even *(name of children's librarian)* to help us kids find the books we're looking for. *(Pauses.)* Hey, Carla, maybe the kids can help us thank our superheroes at the library for all they do.

CARLA: Great idea, Skippy!

SKIPPY: *(To audience.)* Can you kids help us? On the count of three, let's tell the library people, "Thank you! You are my superhero." One, two, three…*(Shouts.)* THANK YOU! YOU ARE MY SUPERHERO!

SKIPPY: Good job, kids! *(To Carla.)* There's something else our library superheroes do.

CARLA: What's that, Skippy?

SKIPPY: They tell us about super days at the library.

CARLA: What's a super day?

SKIPPY: A super day can be a holiday, like Christmas or Easter or George Washington's birthday, or even a day you never heard of, but it's super because they're celebrating it at the library.

CARLA: What super day are they celebrating today?

SKIPPY: Today the library superheroes are going to tell us all about _____. *(Fill in the blank with the holiday, ongoing program you wish to advertise, or even a one-time special event.)*

CARLA: Wow, Skippy! I never knew there was so much happening at the library.

SKIPPY: There's always something new and exciting going on. And with such a great team of superheroes, you know what they say.

CARLA: What?

SKIPPY: Today the library… *(Raises voice and raises hand.)* Tomorrow the world!

CARLA: *(Covers face with hands, then looks at SKIPPY.)* Oh, Skippy, you're too much!

SKIPPY: Come on, Carla. *(Exits, talking.)* Let's go find the other kids and tell them what's happening at the library.

CARLA: I'm right behind you, Skippy. *(Starts to follow, then stops and turns toward audience.)* Hey, I just thought of something. We're superheroes at the library, too. We help out by using our library voice, throwing trash away, being kind to the books, following the rules...

SKIPPY: *(Interrupts from offstage.)* Come on, Carla!

CARLA: *(Exits, pointing up with one arm.)* Super Carla to the rescue!

What Do You Want to Do?

by Cass Crosby

Everyone remembers that libraries are good for informing and educating, but entertainment is just as important. When I was small, we couldn't afford to go to the movies, so we turned to our public library for fun treats: books, movies, computer games. The same thing holds true nowadays, and people constantly seem to rediscover the opportunities for free, fun activities at the local library every time the economy sours.

But don't wait for an economic downturn to remind your audience of that. Of course, if you're sharing this play during your library's Storytime or Puppet Show, you already have an audience smart enough to take advantage of your programming. But you can use it to plug a new program or a one-time event, or help encourage attendance at one that is underperforming.

What Do You Want to Do?
by Cass Crosby

Cast:

TOM: *A typical small boy, spontaneous and dramatic.*

ELLIE: *His more mature friend.*

LIBRARIAN: *Kind and helpful.*

(TOM is onstage, hanging limply over the puppet theater ledge. ELLIE enters.)

ELLIE: What's wrong with you?

TOM: I am SO BORED. I think my brain is numb.

ELLIE: Don't be silly. Summer vacation only just began!

TOM: I spent the last nine months thinking about what I wanted to do once school was out, but now that I have free time, I can't think of anything fun! So here I am, SO BORED and with a numb brain.

ELLIE: Don't let your mom hear that. She'll make you clean your room.

(TOM looks around quickly and straightens up.)

TOM: I'm not that bored. So, what do you want to do?

ELLIE: I don't know. What do you want to do?

TOM: I don't know. What do you want to do?

ELLIE: I'm not bored enough to stand here all day and play *that* game with you. You can't be serious that there's absolutely nothing that you feel like doing!

TOM: Well, I *want* to play my video game, and I *want* to watch TV, and I *want* to play my computer game, but my mom says I already did that this morning, and now I need to do something else. How am I supposed to have fun if I can't watch TV and I can't play my games?

48

ELLIE: No wonder your brain is numb, silly. Tell you what. I was going to the library to pick up a book that came in for me. Do you want to come along?

TOM: Well, okay. Let me tell my mom. *(BOTH exit.)*

(LIBRARIAN is onstage. TOM wanders nearby.)

LIBRARIAN: May I help you?

TOM: My friend is picking up a book, and so I'm left standing here, with my brain numb, and SO BORED. I don't suppose you have anything exciting going on here?

LIBRARIAN: Well, we have books you can check out. What kind of things do you like?

TOM: I like motorcycles! If I had a motorcycle, I wouldn't be bored!

LIBRARIAN: We have books about motorcycles!

TOM: Oh, and I like dinosaurs! If I had a pet dinosaur, there's no way I would be bored!

LIBRARIAN: Oh, you're very lucky! We have books about meat-eating and plant-eating dinosaurs!

TOM: Wow, really! And I like sharks. I saw hammerheads at the aquarium on a field trip!

LIBRARIAN: Yes, we have lots of shark books. But we also have other things. We have computer games you can play, and coloring sheets you can color, and movies you can check out, and all sorts of things.

TOM: Seriously? All that? Here? *(To the audience.)* I think I'm getting dizzy!

LIBRARIAN: And we have programs, too. You can come on _____
for _____. *(Crafts, storytime, summer reading programs, etc.)*

TOM: I think I need to sit down...

LIBRARIAN: Just let me know if you need help finding anything.
I'll be at my desk. *(LIBRARIAN exits. ELLIE enters.)*

ELLIE: Thanks for being patient. Is there anything you wanted to
do here before we go back home?

TOM: Did you know they have motorcycle books here?

ELLIE: Um, yes?

TOM: AND dinosaur books?

ELLIE: Of course. I think they have a whole shelf of them.

TOM: AND shark books?

ELLIE: They have books about lots of different animals.

TOM: AND they do _____ *(crafts, storytime, summer
reading programs, etc.)*?

ELLIE: Yes. They have a calendar, and my mom keeps it on the fridge.

TOM: I didn't know that there was so much to do at the library!
So, what do you want to do first?

ELLIE: I don't know, what do you want to do first?

(TOM and ELLIE start walking slowly offstage.)

TOM: Play on the computer, of course! Oh, wait, no— what if
someone checks out all the good dinosaur books? Hold
on— is that the movie shelf over there?

(BOTH exit.)

I'm Getting a Pet!

by Deanna Baran

Libraries have tons of books about potential pets: not just cats and dogs, but snakes and sugar gliders, bettas and box turtles, canaries and chinchillas, and everything in between.

The problem is, not everyone does their research before choosing a pet. How many people buy a certain breed because they love the way it looks, but don't fully appreciate its specific needs? Perhaps it has the wrong coat for the climate. Perhaps it has more energy than they can keep up with. Or maybe they just had no clue how much grooming it would need.

Whatever the reason, many incompatibilities are predictable and avoidable. Use this play as a gentle reminder that the library is an excellent resource that should be used before making this important decision.

I'm Getting a Pet!
by Deanna Baran

Cast:

BOY: *Knows what he wants to do with a pet, but otherwise doesn't know much about animals.*

GIRL: *Knows enough about animals to tell him when he's wrong.*

(BOY and GIRL are both onstage.)

BOY: Hi, there! Guess what? I'm really excited! My mom's going to take me to the pet store tonight, and I'm going to get a pet! I'm so excited!

GIRL: How fun! What kind of a pet do you want?

BOY: I'm not sure, but I think I want a goldfish. I've always dreamed of having a goldfish to run and play fetch with!

GIRL: You're silly! You can't play fetch with a goldfish!

BOY: Oh. What about a clownfish, like that one in that movie?

GIRL: Nope. You can't play catch with a clownfish, either.

BOY: Oh. Well, how about a guppy? Or an angelfish?

GIRL: You can't play fetch with any kind of a fish!

BOY: Well, drat. Maybe I don't want a pet fish after all. You know, I've always thought hamsters were cool. To be honest, sometimes I can be a little afraid of the dark. It would be great to have a hamster sleeping in my room at night to protect me.

GIRL: Sorry, but there's no such thing as a guard hamster.

BOY: But what if I got one of those scary spiky collars?

GIRL: Nope. Not even then.

BOY: Well, that's no fun! Maybe I don't want a hamster after all. But I think that my best friend's cousin's neighbor has a turtle. I want one, too. I can ride my bike, and my pet turtle can run along next to me! It will keep him in good shape, because no one wants a fat turtle.

GIRL: Turtles don't run!

BOY: Are you sure? I thought a turtle won that race with a rabbit.

GIRL: That was in a story. You can't always believe everything you hear in stories. Some of it's just pretend.

BOY: Well, how can I tell if a story is real or pretend?

GIRL: You can ask a librarian for a book about real animals, like what you would feed your pet turtle, or you can ask a librarian for a book about pretend animals, like bears going on a picnic.

BOY: Would a librarian know a book about a real animal that I can play fetch with, that will help me be brave, and can run with me when I ride my bike?

GIRL: I can't think of an animal like that, but I'm sure a librarian could tell you!

BOY: Then I think I'm going to the library before I go to the pet store!

Feed Your Brain. Read A Book.

by Travis Young

For popularity, few things in the children's section beat trivia books. Whether it's *Ripley's Believe It Or Not* or the *Guinness Book of World Records*, if it deals in the weird, the extreme, the bizarre, kids love it! Take advantage of that natural interest with this play. A little editing will keep it perennially fresh and interesting, even after the umpteenth performance.

Study up on those trivia books yourself, photocopy the script, and pencil in new snippets of information, modifying the dialogue as needed to keep the flow natural. For example, if you ate like a bird, did you know you'd have to eat twice your weight in food? That's a lot of hamburgers!

Do your research. Impress your audience. After all, librarians are professional smart people.

Feed Your Brain. Read a Book.
by Travis Young

Cast:
MILES: *A boy who loves to read.*
RYAN: *A boy who is beginning to realize that books can be interesting.*

Props:
Puppet-sized trivia book, p. 102.

(MILES is onstage, reading a book. Enter RYAN.)

RYAN: Got your nose in a book again, huh?

MILES: Of course! I can learn all kinds of cool things with books.

RYAN: What are you learning about this time? How to talk to your dog? How to fly a helicopter? How to build a catapult for the kitchen table? *(Giggles.)*

MILES: You have to admit, lunch was pretty exciting that day.

RYAN: You've got a point there. Hey, my mom asked me to go to the library and pick up a book for her. Wanna come with me?

MILES: That sounds like fun! I'm almost done with this book, and I'd like another. When are you leaving?

RYAN: Right now. My mom and big brother are both busy, so I have to walk to the library. Can you imagine that! It's like five whole blocks away from my house! And she wants me to walk that far! I wish I was a bird. Then I could just fly.

MILES: Did you know that hummingbirds can fly frontwards?

RYAN: Yeah?

MILES: And backwards?

RYAN: Yeah?

MILES: And upside-down?

RYAN: Yeah?

MILES: But they can't walk?

RYAN: No! Really?

MILES: So there's something that you can do that some birds can't.

RYAN: Wow! That's pretty cool! How did you know that?

MILES: It's in my book.

RYAN: What else is in your book?

MILES: Well, did you know that a cockroach can run in 25 different directions in less than a second?

RYAN: Ha, that's nothing compared to how my big brother drives.

MILES: Maybe it's a good thing you have to walk to the library.

RYAN: You've got a point. *(Pause.)* So what else is in your book?

MILES: Did you know that there are fish that are able to "walk" on their fins? Some of them walk along the bottom of the sea instead of swimming. And some are able to walk on land!

RYAN: Wow! You're kidding, right? I never imagined!

MILES: Yeah. It's a really good book. This is the third time I've read it, but I do have to bring it back to the library so someone else can read it.

RYAN: I think that someone else is going to be me! Come on, let's go!

(BOTH exit.)

Uncle Jonas and the Birthday Bonus

by Mary Ellen Main

Back in the day, access to museums and libraries tended to be extremely limited. Some required letters of introduction from Persons of Quality. Stacks were generally closed to the public. It was almost the 20th century before the first library with a dedicated children's room was built. Things have come a long way towards making libraries accessible and inviting to all.

In this play, Ziggy gets two treats: a book of his very own, and a trip to the library. What can you offer to your patrons to make a trip to *your* library a treat?

Uncle Jonas and the Birthday Bonus
by Mary Ellen Main

Cast:
UNCLE JONAS: *A fun-loving adult.*
ZIGGY: *A curious and excited young person.*

(UNCLE JONAS and ZIGGY are in the middle of a conversation.)

ZIGGY: But what *is* a birthday bonus, Uncle Jonas?

UNCLE: Well, Ziggy, it's like a prize or reward. It's a special treat.

ZIGGY: I love special treats— like ice cream, or candy.

UNCLE: This isn't something to eat. It's much better!

ZIGGY: Better than ice cream and candy?

UNCLE: That's right, Ziggy. And with this special treat, you can keep coming back for more.

ZIGGY: As much as I want?

UNCLE: As much as you want.

ZIGGY: *(Pauses a moment, thinking.)* Is it a pet? I'd love to have a pet. I'd take good care of it. Really I would.

UNCLE: It's not a pet, Ziggy, but it is something you can take good care of. The better you treat it, the longer it will last.

ZIGGY: Uncle Jonas, I still don't know what it is. *(Turns to audience.)* What do you think Uncle Jonas's birthday bonus is? *(Allows time for audience response.)*

UNCLE: It's very special, Ziggy. *(Gives a hint.)* You don't *eat* it, you don't *feed* it, and once you *read* it, you can go back for more.

ZIGGY: *(Thinks, quietly repeating Uncle Jonas's words.)* You don't *eat* it, or *feed* it, and once you *read* it...wait a minute. I know what it is. It's a book!

UNCLE: That's right, Ziggy. Your birthday bonus is a book.

ZIGGY: *(To audience.)* Wow! A book of my very own. *(To Uncle Jonas.)* I can read pictures all by myself, you know.

UNCLE: That's great, Ziggy. And there are many more books at the library that you can look at when you've finished yours.

ZIGGY: Do I get to keep those, too?

UNCLE: No, Ziggy. Library books are for sharing. You take them back so other kids can read them

ZIGGY: Uncle Jonas? *(Pauses, thinking.)*

UNCLE: Yes, Ziggy?

ZIGGY: Well, I was thinking...would you maybe buy me a book again next year for my birthday?

UNCLE: That's a great idea, Ziggy! And if you go to the library, you can find out just what kind of book you would like. Do you want to go pick a book out right now to look at?

ZIGGY: *(Sounds bored.)* No. Not really.

UNCLE: You don't? I thought you were excited about going to the library.

ZIGGY: *(Excited.)* I have a surprise for you, Uncle Jonas.

UNCLE: What's that, Ziggy?

ZIGGY: You know Miss _____, the librarian?

UNCLE: Yes.

ZIGGY: She said I can have two friends come tomorrow and celebrate my birthday at the library.

UNCLE: At the library? *(Pauses.)* What a great idea!

ZIGGY: We can read our picture books to each other...

UNCLE: *(Finishing Ziggy's sentence.)* ...quietly, in the children's corner.

ZIGGY: Of course! Then we can go to my house for an ice cream cake.

UNCLE: I have one more surprise for you, and it's something in a book.

ZIGGY: *(Jumping up and down.)* What is it? What is it?

UNCLE: Well, your mom said we could go to the ice cream store today and pick out what kind of a cake you wanted.

ZIGGY: From a book?

UNCLE: *(Matter-of-factly.)* From a book!

ZIGGY: *(Shaking head, speaks to audience.)* What will they think of next? *(To Uncle Jonas.)* Well, what are we waiting for? Let's go! *(Exits.)*

UNCLE: I'm right behind you. *(Follows Ziggy out.)*

Little Red Riding Hood and the Valentine

by Cass Crosby

Many libraries have a limited stock of puppets with which to work. Many of those are clearly recognizable characters: Little Red Riding Hood is one of the most ubiquitous library puppets. Don't worry about what the audience thinks if she crosses over to do duty in another puppet play!

Small children love recognizable characters, but they also love the thrill of new situations. Import characters whose names and stories they know and love into new plays. Bring together puppets who wouldn't ordinarily meet. Do something fun and unpredictable to keep your audience's interest.

Little Red Riding Hood and the Valentine
by Cass Crosby

Cast:

LITTLE RED RIDING HOOD: *Carrying a Valentine to her grandmother.*
BIG BAD WOLF: *A lonely forest creature who disguises himself as Grandma.*
GRANDMA: *Almost gets her Valentine stolen.*

Props:

Valentine, p. 101.
Covered basket (optional).

(Enter LITTLE RED RIDING HOOD, skipping and humming. Notices the audience, and turns to them.)

RED: Well, hello! I am Little Red Riding Hood, as I'm sure you guessed. See, I have this beautiful riding hood, and it's red, and I wear it all the time. So people call me Little Red Riding Hood. My real name is Gwendolyn Lorraine Lysandra Marinella Rebecca Felicity, but it's a whole lot easier to call me Little Red.

(WOLF peeks over stage from one corner but does not fully come into view.)

RED: *(Continues without noticing him.)* I suppose you wonder what I'm doing on this forest path. Well, as a matter of fact, I have in my basket a Valentine for my dear old grandma, who lives on the other side of the forest! And I have some heart-shaped cookies with pink frosting and sprinkles. I made them myself. The cookies, you see, not the sprinkles. Those came from the store.

(WOLF peeks over stage from other side, but does not fully come into view.)

RED: *(Continues on without noticing him.)* I'm sure my grandma will love the Valentine, and will put it on her refrigerator! And if I'm lucky, she'll ask me to help her eat the cookies. Oh, I hope she does. I loooove heart-shaped cookies with pink frosting and sprinkles. It was nice meeting you! Goodbye!
(LITTLE RED RIDING HOOD exits.)

(Enter WOLF.)

WOLF: Wow! Did you hear that! She's taking her grandma a Valentine and heart-shaped cookies with pink frosting and sprinkles! No one ever brings me cookies. And I've never had a Valentine in my life. I know what I'll do! I'll take a shortcut through the forest, get rid of her grandma, disguise myself, and then Little Red Riding Hood will hand over the Valentine basket without ever knowing the difference! And then I'll finally get a Valentine, and I'll be able to eat heart-shaped cookies with pink frosting and sprinkles! What a great idea!

(Exit WOLF.)

(WOLF, disguised as Grandma, is now onstage. Enter LITTLE RED RIDING HOOD from stage left.)

RED: Grandma! Are you home? It's me, Gwendolyn Lorraine Lys— I mean, it's Little Red Riding Hood!

WOLF: *(In his best Grandma voice.)* Well, hello, Little Red, come in! You crossed the forest just to visit your dear old Grandma! What a good girl you are!

(LITTLE RED RIDING HOOD takes a few steps closer to WOLF, as though coming inside.)

RED: I was making Valentines for my classmates, Grandma, so I thought to bring one for you. And I also made some cookies—

WOLF: *(Interrupts, still in his grandma voice.)* Heart-shaped cookies with pink frosting and sprinkles? My favorites! What a good girl you are!

RED: Er, yes. How did you guess?

WOLF: *(Still in his Grandma voice.)* Because you're such a thoughtful girl, you'd bring nothing less. Now why don't you read me my Valentine?

RED: *(Obviously very proud of her poem.)* Roses are red, violets are purple, dandelions are yellow, but sometimes they're white. Happy Valentine's Day, Grandma. Love, Little Red Riding Hood.

WOLF: *(Not impressed and sounding a little less like Grandma.)* That's it?

RED: *(Hurt.)* What do you mean, "That's it?" It took me a whole hour to make that Valentine! Sure, I was going to go with a "Roses are red, violets are blue" theme, but then I realized that violets are really purple, and the poem kind of changed from there.

WOLF: *(In his ordinary voice.)* I waited my whole life for a Valentine, and that's what I get?!

RED: Hey! You're not my Grandma! You're the big bad wolf who lives in the woods!

WOLF: That's right. I heard you talking to the kids about your basket of cookies and your Valentine, and I wanted them for myself. So I went through the trouble of getting your grandma out of the house for a couple of hours, just long enough for me to trick you. And for that?

RED: You ought to be ashamed of yourself. You can't just steal someone else's Valentine and pretend it's yours!

WOLF: You can't?

RED: No!

WOLF: This isn't the first time I tried to steal a Valentine, you know. But it never works out. I never get any good ones.

RED: Oh? What happened last time?

WOLF: There were these three pig brothers, and I tried to steal their Valentines to each other. But it turned out that one Valentine was made of straw, one Valentine was made of sticks, and the last Valentine was a poem painted on a brick.

RED: You're kidding. Well, Mr. Wolf, if you really want a Valentine, I've still got some leftover construction paper. I can make a Valentine just for you. You don't have to go stealing my Grandma's.

WOLF: You'd do that for me? Even after I tried to trick you?

RED: I'd do that for you. Even though you insulted my poem.

WOLF: I suppose it would be too much to ask if you had any heart-shaped cookies with pink frosting and sprinkles to spare.

RED: Don't push your luck, Mr. Wolf. Now, why don't you run back to your house, and I'll bring your Valentine when I pass by on my way back through the woods?

WOLF: Oh, thank you, Little Red Riding Hood! You're such a good girl! *(Exit BIG BAD WOLF. His voice drifts from offstage.)* Imagine! A Valentine! For me! I'm so excited!

RED: Poor guy. Imagine, going through all that effort for a Valentine!

(Enter GRANDMA.)

GRANDMA: Little Red! You came early! That nice Mr. Wolf told me you were on your way, so I had just enough time to go pick up a box of Valentine chocolates for you. Happy Valentine's Day, dear!

RED: Oh, Grandma! You're so sweet. I have a Valentine for you, too. It goes like this. *(Recites.)* Roses are red, violets are purple, dandelions are yellow, but sometimes they're white. Happy Valentine's Day, Grandma. Love, Little Red Riding Hood.

GRANDMA: Oh, what a marvelous Valentine! I'll be sure to put it on my refrigerator. Are those heart-shaped cookies with pink frosting and sprinkles that I see in your basket?

RED: I made them myself! The cookies, not the sprinkles. The sprinkles came from the store.

GRANDMA: Oh, my! You'll have to help me eat them.

RED: Wow, thanks, Grandma! Say, I need your help, too. I need to make a Valentine for Mr. Wolf, but I can't think of a good poem for him. Can you help me think of one?

GRANDMA: It's probably best to stick with the classics. *(Pauses, thinking.)* How about, "Roses are red, violets are blue, sugar is sweet, Happy Valentine's Day to you?"

RED: I'm sure he'll love that, Grandma.

Pot of Gold

by Daniel Munson

Librarians spend so much time encouraging others to read, it can be easy to neglect your own reading. That's not to say that librarians never read— but often times, we tend to read for others. It's a daunting task. If I had wanted to get into a field that would let me read solely for myself, I could have become a night-shift receptionist instead.

When you were younger, chances were you had a book you loved so much that you re-read it endlessly. The specific title may have changed with time, but chances are, you always had a book or two that you never tired of. How many of us have a book like that now?

In your efforts to encourage literacy in your community, don't forget to treasure a special book of your own.

Pot of Gold
by Daniel Munson

Cast:

STEVIE: *An energetic youth full of imagination. Can be a puppet of any sort, but should be wearing something green, even if it's only a piece of green yarn pinned to him.*

AARON (or **ERIN**): *Another youth, friend to Stevie. Also a puppet of any sort.*

(STEVIE rushes into view and looks around.)

STEVIE: Where is he? Where is that little rascal? He has to be around here!

(AARON enters.)

STEVIE: Watch out! Don't step on him!

(AARON hops and looks around.)

AARON: On who? On what? What are you doing, Stevie?

(STEVIE doesn't answer AARON; he is too busy looking around.)

STEVIE: I thought I saw him come in here. He must be here.

AARON: Stevie?

STEVIE: Lift your foot, Aaron. *(AARON leans to one side and STEVIE looks down at his feet.)* Hmmm. Now your other foot.

AARON: Can I put this one down?

STEVIE: Do you have to?

AARON: Yes!

STEVIE: Well, okay then. *(AARON starts to shift to the other foot.)* But be careful!

AARON: Okay! Don't scare me!

STEVIE: *(Looks down.)* Nope, he's not under your feet.

AARON: What are you looking for?

STEVIE: A leprechaun!

AARON: A 'lepper-what?'

STEVIE: A leprechaun. It's a fairy that looks like an old man.

AARON: Why would he be under my feet?

STEVIE: Because he's really small, and when he's not playing tricks on people, he fixes shoes.

AARON: And is he in here now?

STEVIE: I thought I saw something come in here, and today is the best day to see a leprechaun.

AARON: It is? Why?

STEVIE: It's Saint Patrick's Day! See, I'm wearing green!

AARON: Do you mean you can only catch a leprechaun when you're wearing green?

STEVIE: No. You can catch one any time. If you're lucky. But St. Patrick's Day is a holiday that comes from the country Ireland, and leprechauns come from Ireland too, so they like to come out and celebrate.

AARON: Wow.

STEVIE: And you wear green because…well, you just do when you celebrate an Irish holiday!

AARON: But why are you trying to catch the leprechaun?

STEVIE: That's the best part! They say that if you catch a leprechaun, he'll tell you where he hides his pot of gold.

AARON: A pot of gold!?

STEVIE: Yeah! I guess they must fix a lot of shoes if they have a whole pot of gold to hide!

AARON: What are we waiting for? Let's find that leprechaun!

(STEVIE and AARON move around, looking and calling out.)

STEVIE: Where are you, Mr. Leprechaun?

AARON: Come out, come out wherever you are!

STEVIE: You can fix my shoes!

(AARON stops and looks out at the audience.)

AARON: Wait a minute! I think I see one!

STEVIE: Where?

AARON: Right there! In the front!

STEVIE: *(Points.)* There?

AARON: Yes! You sneak up on the left, and I'll sneak up on the right and we'll grab him. Be careful! He looks crafty!

(AARON starts to sneak out.)

STEVIE: Wait a minute! That's not a leprechaun!

AARON: It's not?

STEVIE: That's a little girl!

AARON: A little … girl?

(AARON looks at the girl, then to STEVIE, out to the girl again, then back to STEVIE.)

AARON: Are you sure?

STEVIE: Don't you know the difference between a little girl and an old man?

AARON: Doesn't an old man have a mustache and beard?

STEVIE: Sometimes.

AARON: Then what's that under her nose?

(STEVIE looks.)

STEVIE: That's a smile and a giggle, not a mustache and beard!

AARON: Oh. Well, let's keep looking then!

(STEVIE and AARON look some more, calling out for the leprechaun. AARON stops to stare at the girl a few times, to make sure it really is a little girl and not the leprechaun.)

STEVIE: Wait a minute! I know where to look!

AARON: Where?

STEVIE: A pot of gold is a treasure, right?

AARON: Right!

STEVIE: What's your best treasure?

AARON: Oh, that's easy. My favorite book is my best treasure.

STEVIE: Mine, too! And where can you find a lot of books?

AARON: In the library!

STEVIE: Libraries are great places to find treasures!

AARON: Then let's go to the library and discover more treasures.

STEVIE: And maybe a leprechaun.

(STEVIE and AARON start to exit.)

AARON: Stevie, do you think that I can get my shoes fixed there, too?

STEVIE: You're not wearing any.

(STEVIE exits. AARON looks down, shrugs, then exits.)

AARON: Here I come, treasured books!

The Imaginary Egg Hunt

by Nikki Loftin

Reading habits tend to drop off around the third grade, and researchers want to know why. They find that reading tends to be more social when children are smaller, but grows into a solo event as they grow older. Likewise, young children's books are well-illustrated, but the older the reader becomes, the more the reader is required to depend on his or her imagination. For children with vivid imaginations, this presents no problem, but for others, this can make reading very difficult.

If you feel like you're losing your readers as they grow older, ask yourself two things: what can you do to help make reading more social, and what can you do to help them grow their imaginations?

The Imaginary Egg Hunt
by Nikki Loftin

Cast:
WINIFRED: *Clarence's serious, taller friend.*
CLARENCE: *Younger, very imaginative, funny.*

Props:
An empty basket for CLARENCE to hold.
A matching basket full of wildly decorated Easter eggs. (Striped, polka-dotted, bright: can be construction paper instead of real eggs.)
A giant construction paper egg, extravagantly decorated. (See pp. 103-104.)

(WINIFRED is on stage. CLARENCE enters, carrying the empty Easter basket.)

CLARENCE: *(Looking around.)* I know there has to be one around here somewhere. Aha! There it is! *(He picks up something invisible.)* That's the most beautiful one yet! Check out those purple and red stripes!

WINIFRED: *(Looking confused.)* Um, Clarence? What are you doing?

CLARENCE: I'm on an Easter egg hunt, Winifred! Want to join me?

WINIFRED: Well, Clarence, normally I would say yes. I love Easter egg hunts. In fact, I hate to brag, but I used to be really, really good at it. I won a chocolate bunny as tall as you when I was a kid, just for finding the most eggs in our town Egg Hunt. I guess you could say I'm kind of an expert at egg hunts. So trust me when I tell you: You're doing it wrong.

CLARENCE: Wrong? What are you talking about? *(He swipes another invisible egg, from right behind Winifred.)* Oh my gosh! Be careful! You almost stepped on one! Look at it. It looks just like a sunrise, all pinky-bluey-goldy. Gorgeous! *(He places it carefully in his basket.)*

WINIFRED: No, seriously, Clarence. What are you doing?

CLARENCE: Um. I told you. I'm on an egg hunt. You can join me: I'll let you use my basket.

WINIFRED: *(Shaking her head, addresses the audience.)* Poor thing. Thinks he's hunting Easter eggs. I'll have to straighten him out. *(To Clarence.)* Okay, you DO have a basket.

CLARENCE: Yes, an Easter basket. I got it last year from my mom.

WINIFRED: And you ARE looking for something—possibly eggs— I'll agree with you on that.

CLARENCE: Looking and FINDING, Ms. Winifred. Looking and finding. Hey, look! There's one over there in the corner! *(Races across the stage and holds up another invisible egg.)* It's zebra-striped! Cool!

WINIFRED: *(Shaking her head.)* No, Clarence. That's your problem, right there. There's nothing in your hand. It's empty.

CLARENCE: Nothing in my hand? What are talking about? Are you sick? Feeling woozy? Did you eat breakfast? Maybe you should see a doctor.

WINIFRED: *(Yelling.)* Me? I don't need to see anybody! I'm fine! It's you! Look. There is nothing. In. Your. Hand. It is empty. Your basket? Empty. You aren't hunting Easter eggs. Because there aren't any eggs here!

CLARENCE: Ohhhhhhhkaaaaaay, calm down, Winifred. I think I know what your problem is.

WINIFRED: I don't have a problem, I've been telling you that—

CLARENCE: *(Shaking his head now.)* Of course not. That's not what I meant. I just meant that you've got the wrong idea. Let me explain: I'm not hunting regular Easter eggs. I'm hunting special Easter eggs.

WINIFRED: Special Easter eggs? What in the world do you mean? Real eggs? The hard-boiled kind? The plastic ones full of candy? Giant ones? What?

CLARENCE: No, no. These are WAY more special than those. Those are all normal eggs. Sure, they're good eggs, *(to audience)* especially the ones stuffed full of chocolate and jelly beans, the red jelly beans are my favorite, and then the blue ones...

WINIFRED: Can you get back to the point, Clarence?

CLARENCE: What? Oh, sure. I'm hunting the most wonderful kind of Easter eggs of all, the most beautiful, glorious, fantastically phenomenal eggs ever! I'm hunting... *(pauses, then whispers)* invisible eggs.

WINIFRED: What did you say?

CLARENCE: *(Louder.)* I'm hunting invisible Easter eggs. Oh look! There's another one, way up there! Can you reach it for me? You're taller.

WINIFRED: No, I can't reach it! There's no such thing as invisible Easter eggs! What a bunch of hooey. You're making all this up, aren't you!

CLARENCE: Of course I'm making it up! *(Shaking head.)* Invisible Easter eggs are super special— because they're imaginary eggs! They're the very best eggs I can imagine. And I hate to brag, but I've been imagining things for years—I had the most exciting imaginary friends in my pre-school for three years running— and these eggs are outstanding.

WINIFRED: Imaginary Easter eggs.

CLARENCE: *(Nodding.)* Yep. Can't you see them?

WINIFRED: No, of course not. There's nothing there! They're not real!

CLARENCE: You can't see them? That's sad! *(To audience.)* Isn't that sad? Oh, poor Winifred. Your imagination must be broken.

WINIFRED: My imagination is just fine.

CLARENCE: No, it must be broken. And that's awful, because it means you won't be able to hunt eggs with me, and I just KNOW the very best imaginary Easter egg is still out there somewhere... The egg of eggs, the prize-winning, monster egg from Egg-olopolis, the capital of Easteralia...

WINIFRED: Did you say... prize-winning?

CLARENCE: *(Sighs.)* Yes, it's the most magnificent egg that's ever been imagined. And your poor imagination's broken, and you'll never... even... be able... to see it. *(Breaks into sobs.)*

WINIFRED: Come to think of it, that is really sad. I wish I could see that egg. I'm a really good egg hunter. I could probably help you find it. If it was really real, of course. *(Mutters.)* Bunch of nonsense, imaginary invisible Easter eggs...

CLARENCE:*(Yells.)* Wait! I've got! We'll fix your imagination.

WINIFRED: Fix it? How?

CLARENCE: Close your eyes! *(Waits.)* Come on, close them. No peeking.

WINIFRED: Fine. I closed them. *(Covers eyes with hands, or ducks head.)* Now what?

CLARENCE: I want you to imagine the most gorgeous, colossal Easter egg you can, bigger than any egg ever, bigger than an ostrich egg. Can you see it?

WINIFRED: A really big egg. Sure, sure. I got it. What is it? What is it?

CLARENCE: Now paint it. Not just one color. Use every color you can. Use colors that haven't even been invented. Make polka dots, stripes, curlicues... keep going until it's all done, completely done. Make it the most beautiful egg ever, a masterpiece, a work of art! Got it?

WINIFRED: *(Excited.)* Yes! Yes! I can see it! It's wonderful!

CLARENCE: *(Looks around.)* That's weird. I don't see it yet. *(Looks out at audience.)* Hey! I know what's wrong. You're not imagining it! Go ahead, all you people. Close your eyes. No peeking. I see you peeking over there. It's not going to work until you all have your eyes closed. Big kids, too. Okay. Now everyone imagine... imagine... imagine... imagine... *(While eyes are shut, Clarence's basket is replaced by the basket full of decorated eggs, and the enormous Easter egg appears at the back or side of the stage.)* Oh, WOW! Winifred! Your imagination is fixed!

WINIFRED: *(Uncovers eyes.)* Everyone look! It's wonderful! It's the most awesome egg ever!

CLARENCE: You see? The imagination is a powerful thing. Now do you believe that I was hunting eggs?

WINIFRED: I believe you, Clarence. Can I hunt, too?

CLARENCE: Sure! You can share my basket. I have to say, I'm really impressed with your enormous egg. Did you imagine that all by yourself?

WINIFRED: Well, I had a little help. Not that I like to brag—but I always have been particularly good at all things Easter egg-y. Hey look! I see a purple and pink one over there!

(The two puppets rush off stage, excitedly picking up invisible eggs on their way.)

Something Delicious

by Lynn Garza

I remember the patron who came in one day, looking for a book for her fourth-grade son. I asked her for the last book he read. *"War and Peace,"* she proudly told me. And the last book he had read for fun? That was *My Teacher is an Alien.*

Sometimes it can be hard for parents— and librarians— to remember what we want kids to like isn't necessarily what they themselves are attracted to. I know one fifth grader whose favorite book is *Jane Eyre;* another's speed is more along the lines of *Goosebumps.*

It's good to encourage kids to expand their boundaries and expose them to new things, but it's equally important to respect their tastes. Let them have their ice cream cones when they want them, but it's important to let them know that chocolate cherry bombes exist in the world, too.

Something Delicious
by Lynn Garza

Cast:

JAMIE: *He thinks it's a simple question, but soon realizes he's out of his depth.*

LIBRARIAN: *Eager to share her love of all things gastronomic with a curious patron, she delivers her lines with the enthusiasm of a cooking show host.*

Ballpark Pronunciation:

Chicken cordon bleu: CHICK-en COR-don BLUH

Très délicieux: TRAY deli-SHOE

Bombe: BOM

JAMIE: I was wondering if you could help me find a book, please.

LIBRARIAN: We have lots of books at the library! What kind of book would you like?

JAMIE: Mother's Day is coming up. My mom makes the best peanut butter and jelly sandwiches in the world for me, so I wanted to make something delicious for her. I was wondering if you had any books that told you how to make food.

LIBRARIAN: Those are called cookbooks, and we have lots of them here! Does your mom trust you in the kitchen?

JAMIE: My big sister promised me that she would help me if I brought her a book that told her how to make what I wanted.

LIBRARIAN: Excellent! It's important to have permission before you do anything in the kitchen. Now, let's see... do you know what kind of delicious food you want to make for her?

JAMIE: I don't really know. If you find something you like, my mom will probably like it, too. What do you suggest?

LIBRARIAN: *(Pretends to look around a bookshelf.)* Well, here's an excellent recipe for chicken cordon bleu. Lots of people find it very delicious!

JAMIE: Chicken what?

LIBRARIAN: Chicken cordon bleu. It's French. You have chicken rolled around ham and Swiss cheese, often dredged in breadcrumbs, swimming in a creamy wine sauce... Très délicieux!

JAMIE: I don't know about that. It sounds a little weird. Do you have anything more normal?

LIBRARIAN: *(Musing while looking for the next book.)* You're right. That might be a little ambitious. Well, perhaps pizza might be more up your alley?

JAMIE: Oo! Pizza!

LIBRARIAN: Yes! Here's a recipe for oven-baked pizza with caramelized onions, gorgonzola, and walnuts. Yum, yum, yum! Can't you smell it already!

JAMIE: I know my mom likes pepperoni, but I don't think she's ever put nuts on her pizza. Is there anything else?

LIBRARIAN: Well, maybe that IS a little exotic. Let me see... *(Pretends to search through more volumes.)* Maybe something dessert-y might be a little safer. Ah! Here we go. How about a chocolate cherry bombe?

JAMIE: *(Alarmed, with a tinge of skepticism.)* A bomb? Now you're joking with me.

LIBRARIAN: Not a bomb; a bombe. More French. You pack ice cream or mousse into a round mold and freeze it. Cherry ice cream mixed with nuts and chocolate wafers, coated with a smooth chocolate shell... oh, dear me. If you don't check this one out, I think *I* will. That looks delicious!

JAMIE: That's okay. You can have it; we usually just eat ice cream from a cone.

LIBRARIAN: I'm so sorry I haven't found a recipe that you like. That's the funny thing about food: everyone's idea of what's delicious is different. But then again, everyone's idea of a good book is different, too. But keep looking, because there's something out there for everyone.

JAMIE: Well, I was kind of thinking...

LIBRARIAN: Yes?

JAMIE: Do you have any recipes for how to make a peanut butter and jelly sandwich?

LIBRARIAN: A peanut... butter... and jelly... sandwich.

JAMIE: Yes. I don't know how, because my mom always makes them. But she makes them taste so good!

LIBRARIAN: Err... yes. I think we do have a book like that. Follow me, please!

(BOTH exit.)

A Costume For Dad

by JoLyn Brown

At our library, Halloween was always a delicate holiday. Many of our patrons weren't comfortable with it, and would discreetly stay home whenever we scheduled a Halloween-themed storytime. Several others were okay with dressing up their children in costumes and letting them trick-or-treat in our parade, but didn't want anything to do with witches, goblins, and ghosts.

If you have a similar demographic, you can easily modify this play to suit local taste. Instead of Dad experimenting with the witch's hat and the ghost costume, come up with more innocuous costumes for him to attempt.

A Costume for Dad
by JoLyn Brown

Cast:
SON: *A small boy eager to share Halloween with his father.*
DAD: *In it for the candy.*

Props:
One small black witch's hat.
One ghost costume.
One candy-wrapper costume.
One candy-wrapper hat.
(See pp. 105-111 for stick puppet templates.)

SON: Dad, why don't you have a Halloween costume?

DAD: Halloween? What's that?

SON: Don't you know, Dad? It's the day we dress-up as ghosts, pumpkins, firefighters and stuff. Then we get candy.

DAD: Oh, that day. Well, I'm too old; no one gives old guys candy on Halloween.

SON: You aren't too old; you just don't have a costume.

DAD: Is that right?

SON: Yes. Don't you know anything about Halloween, Dad? Didn't you go to preschool and learn about it when you were small?

DAD: Yes, but it's hard to remember that far back.

SON: Okay, then I will have to help you. You can't be a firefighter because that's what I'm going as. Do you want to try on the witch's hat?

DAD: Sure. *(Dad puts on the witch's hat.)*

SON: *(Laughing hard.)* Dad! That hat is too small. You look silly.

86

DAD: Well, I wouldn't make a good witch anyway. I don't have long hair.

SON: That's okay; we can keep looking.

DAD: Oh good. *(Removes hat.)*

SON: Hmm. Wait! I know, you can be a ghost!

DAD: *(Sounds unsure.)* If you think so. *(DAD puts on the ghost costume. It is too small and he can't see. He stumbles around, bumping into things.)* Oh, no! I can't see! Son! Son! Where are you?!

SON: *(Yelling and dodging DAD.)* Dad, you have to look through the holes for your eyes!

DAD: What holes? *(He trips.)* Humph. Son, I don't think we have any costumes that fit me. *(Removes ghost costume.)*

SON: Don't worry. I'll think of something.

DAD: Well, let me know if you think of something. I have to go rake leaves. I'll be outside.

SON: Okay. *(Exit DAD. SON turns to the audience.)* This isn't good. What will Dad be for Halloween? He really likes candy. I know because Mom told him to stop sneaking the candy because it was supposed to be for the trick-or-treaters. He'll be sad if he doesn't get any. What do you think he should be?

(Let the children give suggestions for what DAD could be.)

SON: Hmm, those are good ideas, but I don't think we have those costumes. Maybe I need to look at the library book my teacher gave me. It's about Halloween and there are lots of costumes in it.

(Exit SON; enter DAD.)

DAD: Son! It's almost time to get your costume on. Where are you?

SON: *(Enters.)* Right here, Dad. I know what you can be for Halloween. I thought of it when I read my Halloween book. I made you the best costume!

DAD: Really? What is it?

SON: Here, put it on!

(DAD puts on the candy costume except for the hat.)

DAD: Wow! This is a really great costume. What am I?

SON: You're Halloween Candy!

DAD: *(Laughing.)* I sure am.

SON: Here, put on your hat.

(DAD puts on the hat.)

SON: You look great!

DAD: Yes I do. But where did you get all these wrappers?

SON: I unwrapped all the candy Mom bought for tonight. It took forever!

DAD: What did you do with the candy?

SON: *(As though stating the obvious.)* I put it back in the candy bowl, Dad.

DAD: Oh. Well, let's get you into your firefighter outfit. I can't wait to see your mom's face when she sees my new costume.

SON: All right! We're going to have the best Halloween costumes of all!

DAD: We sure are.

(BOTH exit.)

Curly Shares in Tradition

by Sarah V. Richard

Christmas is likely to be a major holiday, regardless of your demographics. Whether you wish to present a more circumspect message of peace, love, and goodwill, or if you prefer to be direct and present the story of the Nativity itself, this play lends itself to either a secular or religious interpretation, depending on your choice of accompanying book. Either way, it provides an opportunity to shift the emphasis of the holiday away from the material— such as presents— and give your audience something more meaningful to consider.

Curly Shares in Tradition
by Sarah V. Richard

Cast:
LIBRARIAN: *Sitting in front of the puppet stage with a book to read.*
CURLY: *A puppet who will interact with the Librarian.*

Props:
A wrapped giftbox with a removable lid, topped with a large bow.

(LIBRARIAN is sitting near the front of the stage with the prop present, in which is contained the day's storybooks. Enter CURLY.)

LIBRARIAN: I'm so excited! This is my favorite time of the year!

CURLY: Me, too. I love Christmas! You get to open lots of presents!

LIBRARIAN: Isn't Christmas great? It's a time to be with family.

CURLY: And open presents.

LIBRARIAN: Everyone sits down together to eat a big meal—turkey, stuffing, gravy, green bean casserole, and pecan pie.

CURLY: And open presents.

LIBRARIAN: We sing Christmas carols.

CURLY: And open presents.

LIBRARIAN: Well, Curly, I think it's safe to say your favorite thing about Christmas is opening presents.

CURLY: I love Christmas! There are so many presents! Is that a present you're holding, Mr./Mrs. _____?

LIBRARIAN: Yes, it is, but before we open this present, I have a question for you. What are some of the Christmas traditions that you and your family have, Curly?

CURLY: What's a tradition?

LIBRARIAN: A tradition is something that your family does every year during the holiday season.

CURLY: *(Scratches head.)* Hmm, I can't think of anything except opening presents.

LIBRARIAN: How about I share a tradition with you? It's something I like to do every Christmas with my family.

CURLY: Okay, what's your tradition?

LIBRARIAN: Every year, before we open presents, my family reads a story.

CURLY: I love reading stories!

LIBRARIAN: And since it's Christmas, we read a Christmas story. Would you like to hear one?

CURLY: Would I like to hear one? Is my hair curly?

LIBRARIAN: I'll take that to mean yes.

CURLY: You betcha! *(Points to box.)* Can we open that present now?

LIBRARIAN: That's a great idea. *(LIBRARIAN lifts the lid off the box and pulls out a Christmas-themed book, such as* 'Twas the Night Before Christmas *or a baby Jesus story.)*

CURLY: Why, it's *(insert book name)*. I love that story. Let's read it.

(LIBRARIAN opens the book and reads the story.)

CURLY: I think I'm going to start a new tradition with my family, too!

LIBRARIAN: I'm glad you liked my idea.

CURLY: Librarians always have good ideas! Hey, I know, maybe we can start a New Year's tradition and start the new year off by reading a New Year's story.

LIBRARIAN: Sounds like you have some good ideas of your own.

CURLY: And on Valentine's Day, we can read a Valentine's story! And on Easter, an Easter story, maybe a Fourth of July story, and a Halloween story, and a Thanksgiving story too!

LIBRARIAN: I'll be looking forward to it.

CURLY: Yeah, I can't wait! *(Waves.)* See you next time!

LIBRARIAN: 'Bye, Curly!

A December Emergency

by Nikki Loftin

It's easy to forget that children process time differently at different stages of their development. Older children are able to think in terms of past and future; younger children are all about the immediate present; and still younger children have their own unique sense of the passage of time.

Take the opportunity to translate time into terms they *can* grasp. Parents might have a special calendar marking down the days to a vacation; some families count down to Christmas with an Advent calendar; visual aids, like an hourglass or timer, help children grasp smaller increments of time.

Christmas can't come fast enough for many children. Help make the wait more manageable and translate days into books.

A December Emergency
by Nikki Loftin

Cast:

MARIAN: *A level-headed librarian.*

PEANUT: *A silly, over-dramatic library patron, who makes far too much noise.*

Props:

Some puppet-sized books.

A wristwatch for Peanut to wear.

(Enter PEANUT, who flops dramatically over the side of the stage.)

PEANUT: *(Yelling.)* Oh! The agony! The agony! The horrible, eternal terribleness of it all!

MARIAN: *(Enters quickly, carrying some books.)* Peanut! Be quiet. You're in a library. People are trying to read!

PEANUT: *(Still yelling, gesturing dramatically.)* I can't be quiet. It's too awful, Marian. It's the Worst Thing Ever.

MARIAN: What's wrong? What's wrong?

PEANUT: You'll never believe it. I can tell you... but you'll Never. Believe. It.

MARIAN: Did your dog run away and join the circus?

PEANUT: No.

MARIAN: Did a giant meteor fall on your house?

PEANUT: No.

MARIAN: Then what happened???

PEANUT: Time. Has. Stopped.

MARIAN: *(Rubbing hand on her head in exasperation.)* You're right, Peanut. I don't believe it.

PEANUT: But I'm not kidding, Marian! Time has stopped.

MARIAN: Okay, Peanut. Tell me why you think time has stopped.

PEANUT: Well, this morning I flipped the page on my calendar, and it said today was December the first.

MARIAN: So?

PEANUT: *(Exasperated.)* How can you say that? Don't you know what comes in December?

MARIAN: Um… snow?

PEANUT: NO!!! Everybody knows what happens in December. It's only the most fun, most awesome, most presenterrific day EVER!!!

MARIAN: Oh, you mean Christmas.

PEANUT: *(Throws hands up in the air.)* Yes, Christmas! But the awful thing is, now Christmas is never going to come… because TIME HAS STOPPED.

MARIAN: But why do you think time has stopped?

PEANUT: Well, when I first realized it was December, and Christmas, the most wonderful day ever, with presents and food and singing, and dancing, and festivities, was right around the corner, I sat down to wait for it to arrive. And— *(dramatic pause)* it never did. In fact, I looked at my watch when I very first started thinking about Christmas, and then I looked at it again when I was POSITIVE I had waited long enough, that 24 days MUST have passed… and you'll never believe it.

MARIAN: Probably not, but go ahead and tell me.

PEANUT: Only two minutes had passed. Two minutes… and I had been waiting for weeks. It had to have been weeks!!

MARIAN: I think you were just excited about Christmas. I don't think time really stopped. I mean, Christmas is pretty exciting. Does anyone here get excited about Christmas? Does it seem like it's always far away? Does is seem like—sometimes, maybe—time is going slower, because it's so hard to wait? *(Waits for audience to respond.)* You see, Peanut? Time hasn't stopped. It's just that waiting for Christmas makes it seem like it's going slower.

PEANUT: *(Flopping down again.)* Oh! Oh! Oh, the agony! The terrible waiting…

MARIAN: Hush, Peanut. We are still in a library. Why don't you take these books about Christmas?

PEANUT: *(Scoffing.)* Why are you giving me books about Christmas, Marian? I already know about Christmas.

MARIAN: Well, one way to make the time go faster is to read. Have you ever heard that time flies when you're having fun? Well, if you like Christmas, you should learn all you can about it! It'll be fun!

PEANUT: No, Marian. I already know EVERYTHING about Christmas.

MARIAN: *(Skeptically.)* Oh, really? Did you know that in Holland, they call Santa Claus *Sinterklaas,* and they give presents on December the fifth? Did you know that in Mexico they celebrate with a piñata full of nuts, and candy, and toys, and that on January 6th they put out shoes instead of stockings for the Day of Kings?

PEANUT: *(Embarrassed.)* Um, no. I did not know those things. Can I see those books, please?

MARIAN: Here. Take seven. That's one book a day, for a week. Then you can come back in and get seven more. And in twenty-four books, it will be...

PEANUT: *(Yells.)* Christmas Day!

MARIAN: Yes, Christmas Day. Now be quiet, and go home, and start reading.

PEANUT: Wait! Do you have enough books to last me until Christmas?

MARIAN: Yes, Peanut. This is a big library, and we have lots of books about Christmas. We'll have enough.

PEANUT: Okay. *(Looks at his watch.)* OH NO!!!

MARIAN: What is it? What is it?

PEANUT: Time just stood still again! My birthday is only 67 days away. That mean I'm going to need— *(speaking to himself)* carry the nine, take away fourteen, take the square root of infinity... I'll need 67 books about my birthday! Can you help me???

MARIAN: *(Sighs.)* I'll see what I can do.

PEANUT: *(Hugs Marian.)* Oh, thank you Marian. You're the best librarian ever!

MARIAN: Thank you, Peanut. And Merry Christmas.

Props
and
Patterns

The Princess' book for *Oh, Dear. Oh, Deer!* on p. 25.
Copy it onto ivory cardstock, cut, and fold.

If you can't find a fly finger puppet, cut this out onto cardstock and attach it to a craft stick with a glue dot. For use with the play on p. 25.

Visit librariansaide.com/puppetpatterns for additional stick puppet templates for this play.

Roses are Red

Violets are Purple

Little Red Riding Hood's valentine for the play on p. 63. Copy it, color it, and dress it up with sparkly glitter.

1,000 aMaZiNg FacTs

Print this onto brightly colored cardstock, cut, and fold.
For use with *Feed Your Brain. Read a Book.* on p. 55.

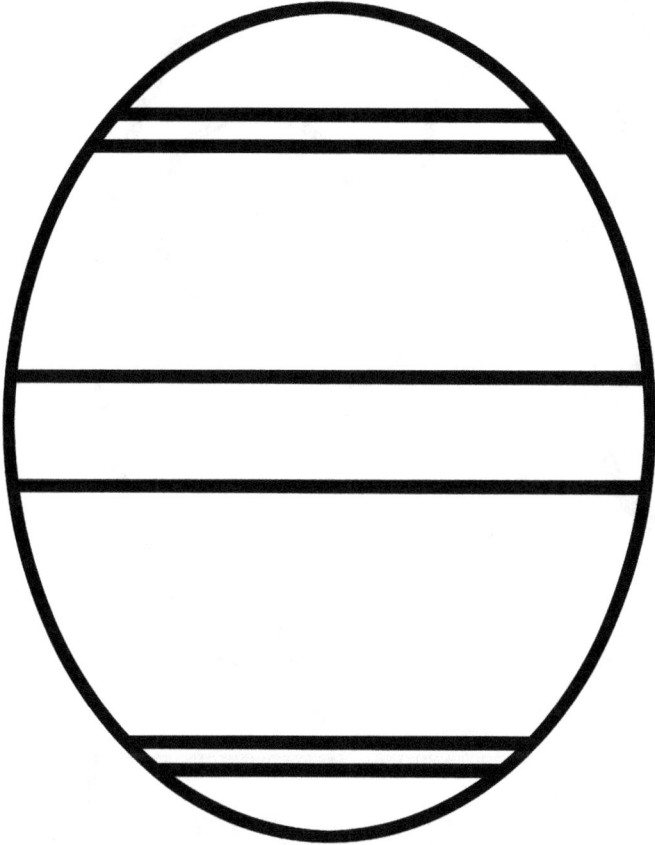

Print several copies of each egg onto cardstock.
Use markers and colored pencils to uniquely decorate each egg.
Use your photocopier to create a larger, special egg,
and decorate that one with glitter, bits of trim,
or other special scraps.
For use with *The Imaginary Egg Hunt* on p. 75.

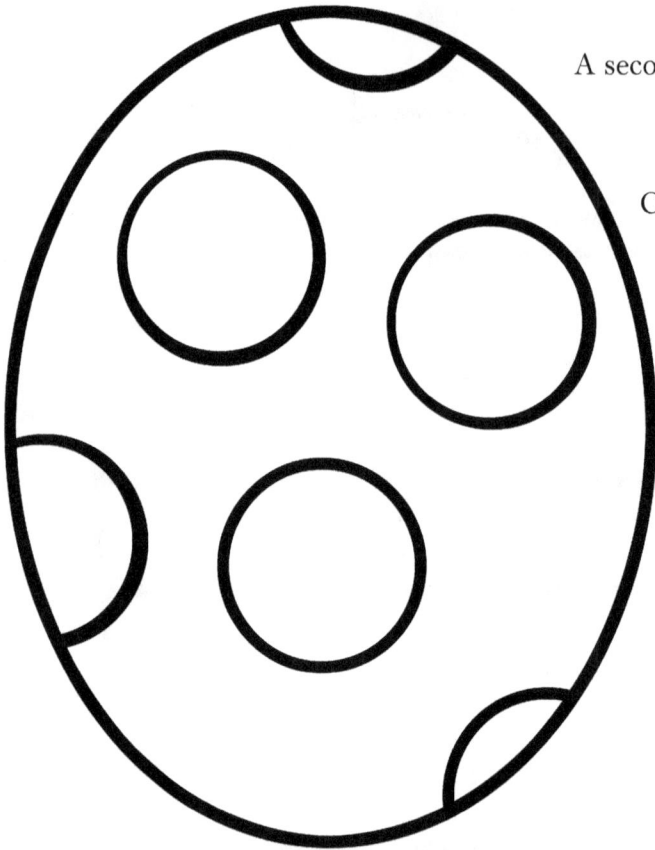

A second pattern for
*The Imaginary
Egg Hunt*
on p. 75.
Create multiple
copies in
different
sizes and
decorate
them
uniquely.

Library Card

Although you're likely to have your own library cards as props,
not all libraries use them.
Print onto stiff paper and attach to puppet's hand
with tape or thread.
For use with *An Exclusive Club* on p. 35.

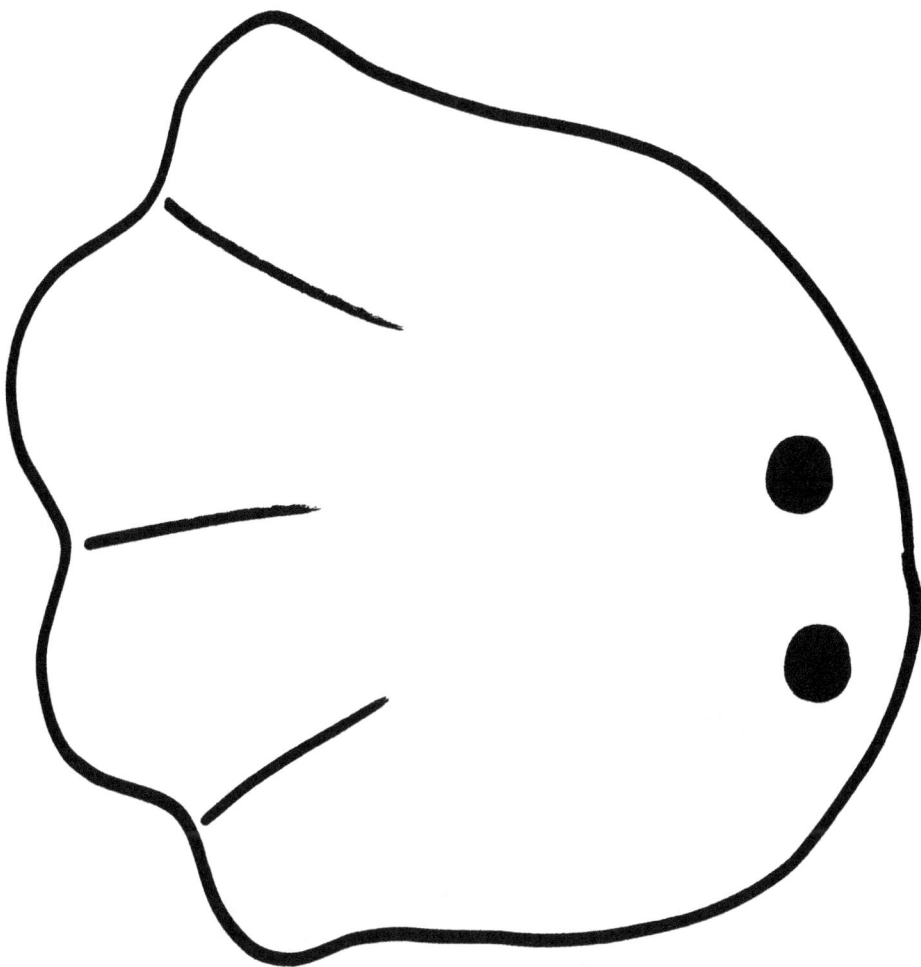

Quick changes can be difficult, especially with a one-person show.
To get around this, make multiple copies of your Dad puppet:
have one uncostumed version on hand,
a second version wearing the witch's hat,
a third copy already dressed in the ghost costume,
and a fourth version wearing the candy outfit.
Alternately, try using bits of velcro to swap out costumes.

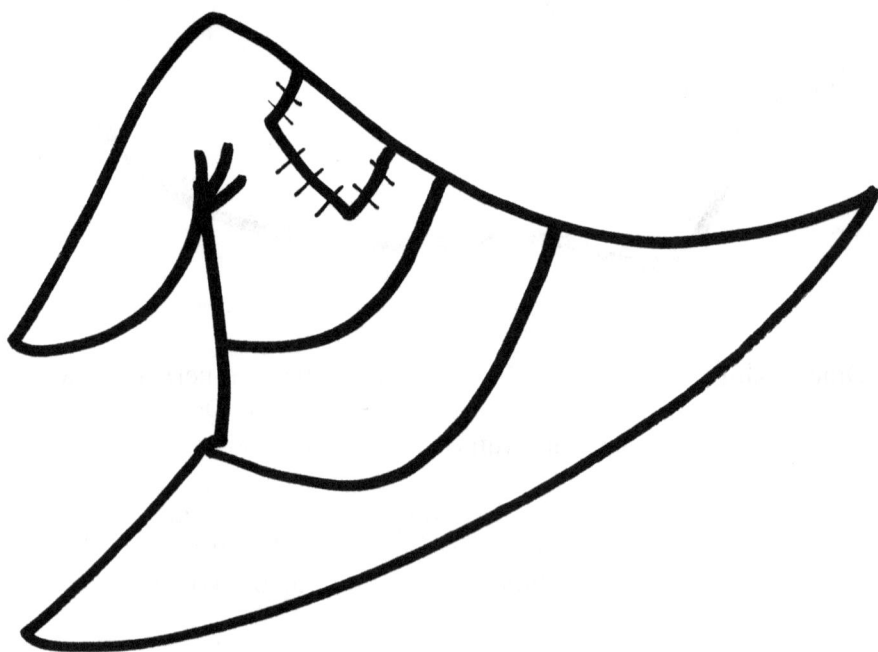

If you have difficulty finding costumes for your hand puppets,
try making stick puppets instead.
Copy the patterns onto stiff cardstock,
color, and cut out. Assemble them with glue dots
and fasten them to a craft stick.
These patterns are for use with the play on p. 85.

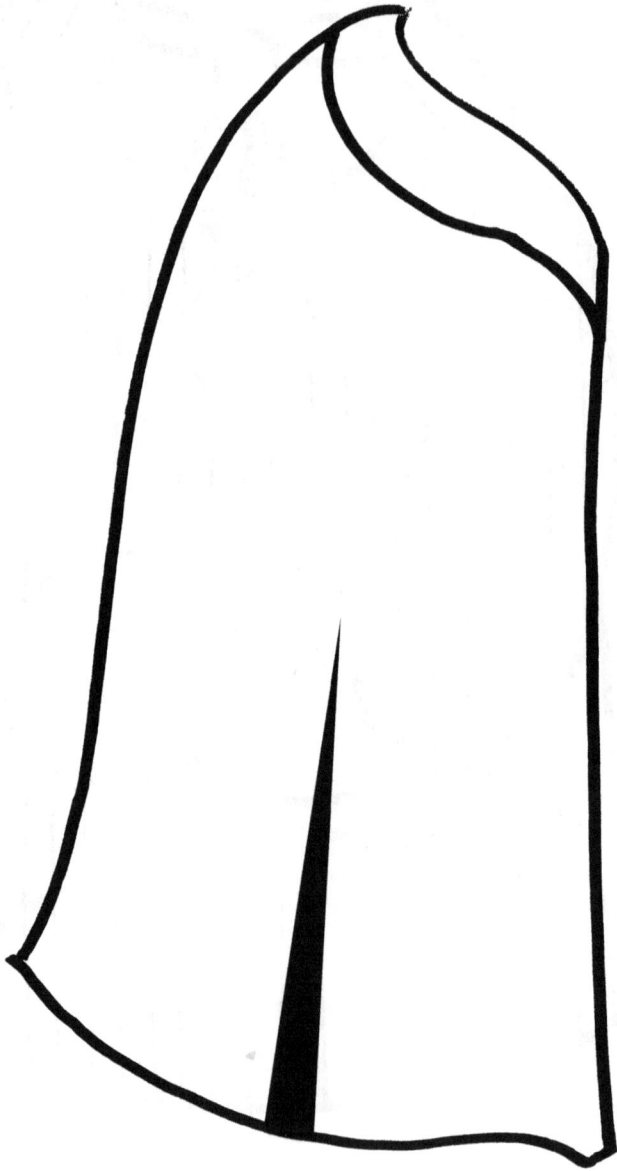

Copy both parts
of the cloak onto
cardstock.
Cut them out
and decorate
the costume
with colorful
candy wrappers.
Consider folding
shiny foil wrappers
into interesting shapes
and fastening them
in colorful patterns
by using glue dots.

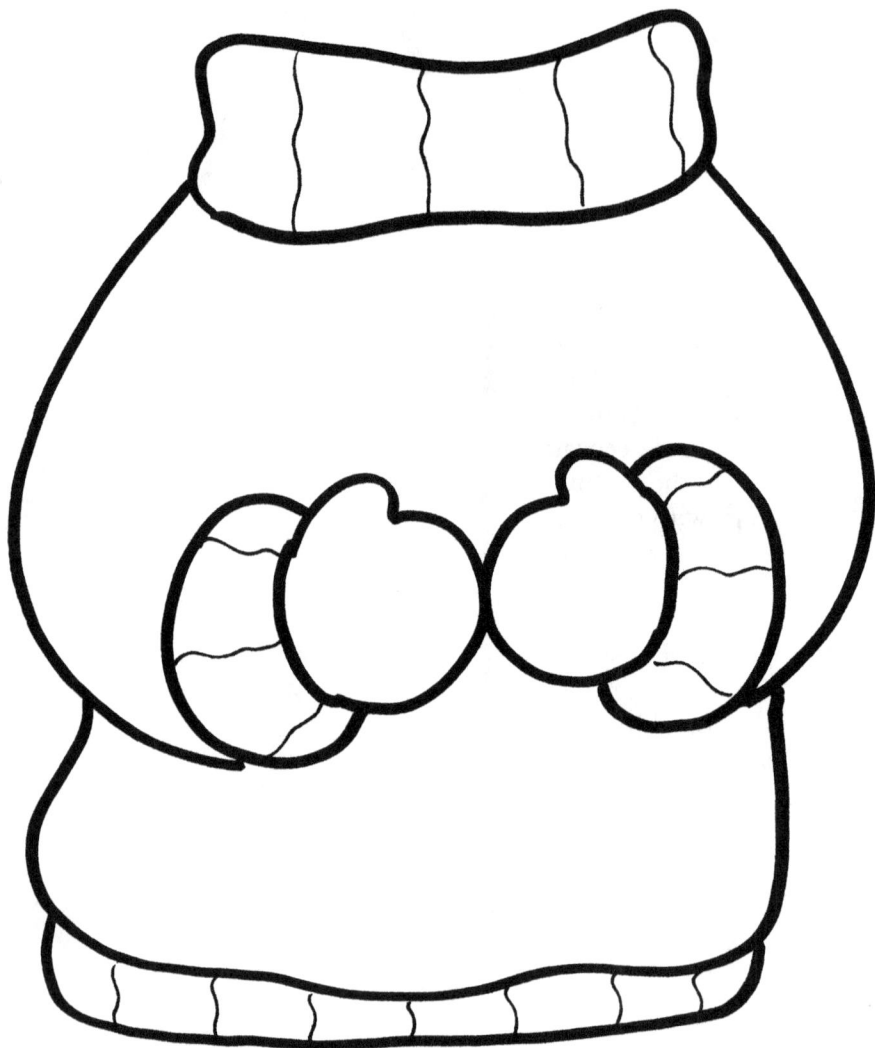

All images between pp. 105-111 are for use
with the play on p. 85, *A Costume for Dad*.

Decorate this hat
to match
the candy cloak
pp. 108-109.

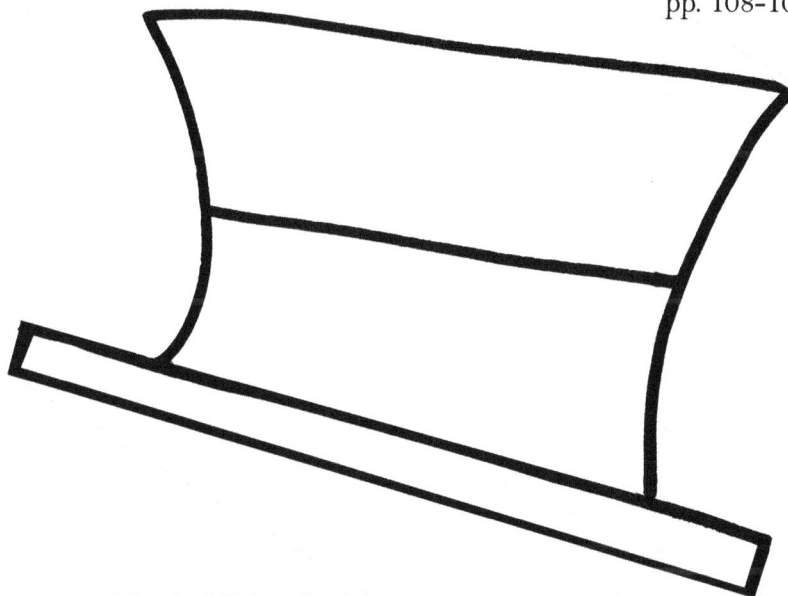

Need additional stick puppet characters?
Visit librariansaide.com/puppetpatterns
and print them from your own computer!

www.ingramcontent.com/pod-product-compliance
Lightning Source LLC
Chambersburg PA
CBHW072202090426
42740CB00012B/2359

9 780984 325108